Emily Dickinson's Gardening Life

Emily Dickinson's Gardening Life

The Plants & Places
That Inspired the Iconic Poet

Marta McDowell

Timber Press • Portland, Oregon

⚘ FRONTISPIECE The single authenticated photographic
image of Emily Dickinson, circa 1847.

Revised edition published in 2019 by Timber Press, Inc.,
a subsidiary of Workman Publishing Co., Inc.,
a subsidiary of Hachette Book Group, Inc.
1290 Avenue of the Americas
New York, NY 10104

timberpress.com

Originally published by McGraw-Hill in 2005 as *Emily Dickinson's
Gardens: A Celebration of a Poet and Gardener*

Printed in China on responsibly sourced paper
Fourth printing 2023

Text design by Hillary Caudle
Jacket art by Montse Bernal
Endpaper image by The Emily Dickinson Museum, Amherst, Massachusetts

ISBN 978-1-60469-822-0

Catalog records for this book are available from the
Library of Congress and the British Library.

FOR KIRKE

"OR IS IT DANCING?"

CONTENTS

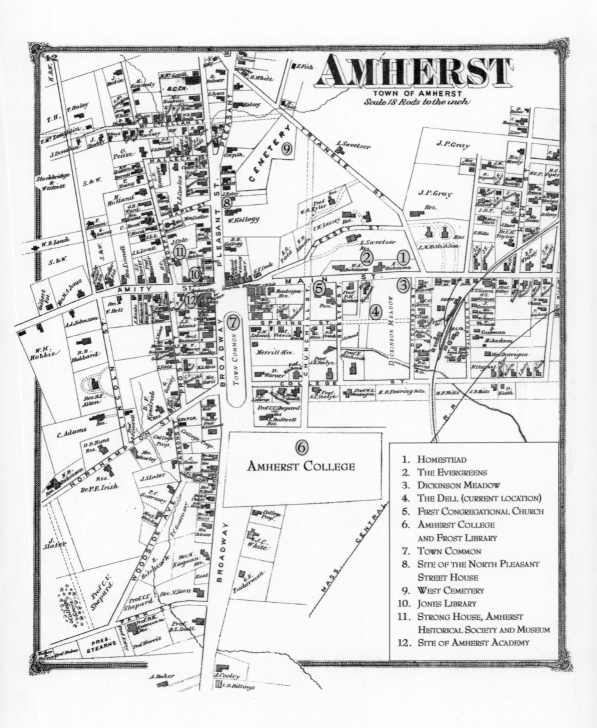

Locations around Amherst connected with Emily Dickinson, overlaid on an 1873 map.

1. HOMESTEAD
2. THE EVERGREENS
3. DICKINSON MEADOW
4. THE DELL (CURRENT LOCATION)
5. FIRST CONGREGATIONAL CHURCH
6. AMHERST COLLEGE AND FROST LIBRARY
7. TOWN COMMON
8. SITE OF THE NORTH PLEASANT STREET HOUSE
9. WEST CEMETERY
10. JONES LIBRARY
11. STRONG HOUSE, AMHERST HISTORICAL SOCIETY AND MUSEUM
12. SITE OF AMHERST ACADEMY

PREFACE TO THE REVISED EDITION

EMILY DICKINSON WAS AN ACCIDENT—for me, at least—in terms of
her gardens and my writing. It occurred in my corporate phase, a
two-plus-decade career that had sprung up, unlikely but fully clothed,
after college graduation. A forty-something me in the guise of diligent
insurance executive was driving solo to agencies across New England
to deliver the latest management message.

It was midafternoon in summer, the 1990s, between a lunchtime
meeting in Framingham, Massachusetts, and an overnight stop in
Springfield. Westbound on I-90, the Mass Pike stretched across the
middle of the state, shimmering in the heat. I was in dire need of caf-
feine. Turn signal. Ludlow Service Plaza. The rest of the day yawned
ahead with the anticipated solitary dinner, anonymous hotel, and too
much email. But as with interstate rest areas from sea to shining sea,
a literature rack beckoned with local tourist offerings. My eyes lit on a
brochure for the Emily Dickinson Homestead.

The heart of a liberal arts major still beat in my suit-clad frame.
Bits of Dickinson's poems fluttered in distant memory, their own
things with feathers. As the museum's brochure listed the last tour at
4:00 p.m., I called from the pay phone, which now seems unspeakably
quaint. A woman with the inflections of mid-Massachusetts said that
yes, I would be able to make it to Amherst in time.

The drive north was bucolic—the Connecticut River with the
Calvin Coolidge Bridge, rolling farmland, an absence of strip malls

and traffic lights. The shady common of downtown Amherst was quiet mid-week in summer with its college students away.

The Dickinson Homestead was an encounter that seemed, well, transcendental. I learned from the guide that, like me, Emily Dickinson was a gardener. Here was her collection of pressed plants, or at least a facsimile. A photograph of her conservatory was framed on the wall of her father's study, the same wall that used to open onto a small glass room with her shelves of potted plants. Stepping out into the wide expanse that was her garden, I started on a much longer road. Her garden became a way for me to learn, to think about her life and her poems in the context of her pursuit of plants. It was Dickinson who brought me to garden writing.

I have Tom Fischer to thank twice for smoothing the way to my pursuit of Emily Dickinson's gardens. It first came in the form of a refusal, in 1999, of an article submission to *Horticulture*, a magazine he then edited. He sent me the nicest rejection letter, suggesting I send the proposal on to David Wheeler at *Hortus*, a British gardening journal for which I still write. Almost twenty years later Tom, by then at Timber Press, and his colleague Andrew Beckman suggested this revised edition.

It is great to have a do-over for anything in life, including a book. For those familiar with the first edition, now long out of print, you will note new material and color illustrations throughout. Revisions incorporate scholarship and research since the first edition, and of course, correct and amend along the way. The new edition is reorganized. The first part of the book focuses on Emily Dickinson's life as a gardener in step with the progression of a year in her garden. The second part includes a visitor's guide to the Dickinson landscape, including the Emily Dickinson Museum, which has seen major changes in the past twenty years. I hope you get a chance to visit or visit again. If you arrange your trip to coincide with one of the museum's garden weekends, perhaps you will come work in the garden with me. If you want to plant a poet's garden of your own, you'll also find an annotated plant list.

Before we begin, a word about spelling, grammar, and punctuation. The poems and quotes from letters that you'll read in this volume are

taken from editions by two Harvard scholars: Ralph W. Franklin—
the numbers after the poems are from his edition—and Thomas H.
Johnson, who carefully deciphered Dickinson's manuscripts to use her
original words, transcribed directly from her pen. If the punctuation is
peculiar or the spelling unusual, know that it was as she wrote it.

And now, to begin. Again.

INTRODUCTION

⬇

EMILY DICKINSON WAS A GARDENER.

When you hear the name "Emily Dickinson," it may bring to mind a white dress or a well-known image of a sixteen-year-old girl staring boldly out of a daguerreotype. Poetry, of course. Probably not gardening.

Emily Dickinson as a gardener doesn't fit with the Dickinson mythology. The myths were based on real phobias of her later years and were also stoked by her first editor, Mabel Loomis Todd, to promote book sales. Since her death in 1886, she has been psycho-analyzed, compared to medieval cloistered mystics, and called "the madwoman in the attic." All she lacked was a cloister.

Beyond the stuff of literary legend, she was a person devoted to her family, with pleasures and pastimes and deep friendships. She shared a love of plants with her parents and siblings. To friends, she sent bouquets, and to some of her numerous correspondents—over one thousand of her letters have been found—pressed flowers.

She collected wildflowers, walking with her dog, Carlo. She studied botany at Amherst Academy and Mount Holyoke. She tended both a small glass conservatory attached to the front of the house and a long flower garden sloping down the spacious east side of the grounds. In winter, she forced hyacinth bulbs and in summer she knelt on a red blanket in her flower borders, performing horticul-ture's familiar rituals.

This book proceeds in calendar fashion, following the seasons. Welcome to Emily Dickinson's gardening year.

Answer July
Where is the Bee -
Where is the Blush -
Where is the Hay?

Ah, said July -
Where is the Seed -
Where is the Bud -
Where is the May -
Answer Thee - me -

Nay - said the May -
Show me the Snow -
Show me the Bells -
Show me the Jay!

Quibbled the Jay -
Where be the Maise -
Where be the Haze -
Where be the Bur?
Here - said the Year -

667, 1863

🌾 A daisy in Emily Dickinson's garden.

The TURNING of the YEAR

Early Spring

A GARDENER'S HOME AND FAMILY

🌱 Violets painted by Clarissa Munger Badger, from a book that Emily Dickinson owned.

IF YOU TAKE A SHORT WALK from the center of Amherst and stand in front of the Homestead, you'll need to use your imagination—what Dickinson called "reverie"—to summon up the landscape as Emily Dickinson knew it in the mid-1800s.

Main Street is an unpaved road. Today's sidewalks, utility poles, parking signs, and fire hydrants disappear, as do the boards that announce this house and its neighbor as destinations for tourists and literary pilgrims. Replace the drone of car engines and tires with the clomp of hooves and the click of tack. Add sleigh bells if the road is packed with snow. Breathe in to catch a trace—more if the day is warm—of earthy, animal odors.

The property of number 280 is separated from Main Street by a double line: a stylish fence of square wooden pickets, painted a shade of ochre to match the house, and a hedge of clipped, evergreen hemlocks. From the front gate, some steps above the ruts of the street, you look south. Houses and businesses vanish, and you gaze over a wide stretch of stubble that each summer will fill in to earn its name, the Dickinson meadow. Beyond that, there is a clear view of Amherst College.

The Dickinson Homestead on Main Street in Amherst, Massachusetts.

The painted brick house behind the fence and hedge is imposing. The Homestead, as it is called, perches on a knoll. The carriage drive curves around it on the west side. A grove of trees along the drive shelters the house from hot winds of summer and Arctic blasts of winter. If you came calling in later years, you would notice the house that Edward Dickinson, Emily's father, built next door for Austin—her older brother—and Austin's bride, Susan.

Emily could look out her bedroom window along the path that connected the two houses and see her niece, nephews, and the neighborhood children playing in the carefully tended grounds of Austin's home. A bed of "Sister Sue's" hollyhocks edges the path in summer.

Behind the Homestead, a large carriage house and barn take up the rear of the property, shaded by large trees. Horses, cows, chickens, and pigs occupy it, providing the household with transportation, milk, and meat. In front of one wing of the barn, Mrs. Dickinson grows her prize-winning figs. Grapes are trellised there too. A substantial orchard of fruit trees—apples, pears, and cherries—grows down the slope.

Continuing past the barn, you finally see Emily Dickinson's flower garden on the east side of the house. A path of heavy granite flagstone

VIEW OF AMHERST, MASS.

PUBLISHED BY JOHN BACHELDER.

⚘ ABOVE The town of Amherst as seen from the Amherst College hill, circa 1857.

⚘ RIGHT The Evergreens, home of Emily Dickinson's brother and sister-in-law and their three children.

leads down a modest slope through the lawn, alongside fruit trees and flower beds. Lily-of-the-valley carpets some borders, perfuming the spring. Hedges of peonies lend their massive display to May. Honeysuckles sweeten the air from trellises. Roses, awaiting their June cue, clamber over a summer house. Masses of spring bulbs, hyacinths and daffodils, are followed by a profusion of annuals and perennials: sweet peas, nasturtiums, lilies, and marigolds, to name a few. Her niece, Mattie, described it as "a meandering mass of bloom."

A piazza overlooks the west side of the property, just outside the parlor; glass doors open onto it. Today we might call it a deck, but then the style was Italian and romantic. Potted plants like oleander and pomegranate, which would have withered outdoors in a

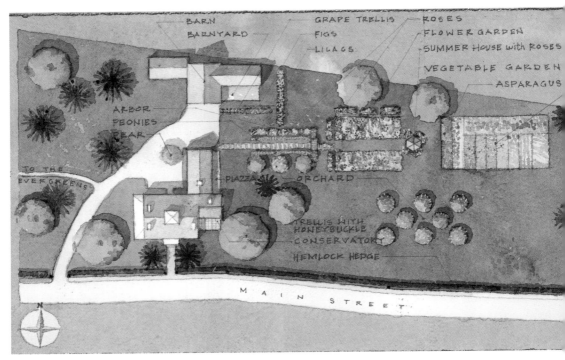

A conceptual map of the Homestead landscape, based on Emily Dickinson's descriptions and the recollections of friends and family.

Massachusetts winter, blossom there in summer. It is easy to picture the Dickinson sisters, Emily and Vinnie, sitting on the piazza in fine weather. They enjoyed the ultimate gardener's reward—those rare moments of surveying one's handiwork after the hard work is done, like the Creator's seventh day enumerated in their King James Bible.

A GARDEN EXISTS IN A PLACE. Amherst, Massachusetts, was the backdrop for Emily Dickinson's garden. The first people of the land— Pocomtuc, Wampanoag, Mahicans—encountered European fur traders in the 1600s exploring the broad reaches of the Fresh River, as the Dutch called the Connecticut. Known today as a college town, Amherst was founded in the mid-1700s by agrarian colonists who appreciated its alluvial soils in what is aptly called the Pioneer Valley. Emily once told her brother that Amherst "seems indeed to be a bit of Eden."

Plants flourish here, in addition to poets. Amherst lies on a fertile fan of land due east of the Connecticut River, eighty miles inland from Boston. In the nineteenth century, it was a landscape of hills and streams, wildflowers and fields.

The fields were farmed. Dickinson's Amherst was a market town, and many of her neighbors were farmers. Everyone who had the means, including gentlemen like her father, planted an orchard and vegetable garden to enrich the summer table and the winter larder. In her first published poem, a valentine, Dickinson wrote:

> Put down the apple Adam
> And come away with me
> So shal't thou have a pippin
> From off my Father's tree!
>
> From 2A, 1852

Built in proper Federal style in 1813 by Edward's father, Samuel Fowler Dickinson, the Homestead was the axis of Emily's world. She was born in one of its upstairs bedrooms, lived and gardened there for forty of her fifty-five years, and died there. It temporarily passed out of the Dickinson family after her grandfather went bankrupt, overextending his credit in establishing a new school—Amherst College. In 1840, when Emily was nine years old, Edward Dickinson and Emily Norcross moved with their three children and set up housekeeping in a spacious white clapboard home on North Pleasant Street. That house was demolished in the 1920s.

Edward, a prominent attorney like his father and treasurer of Amherst College, reacquired the Homestead in the 1850s. The property included two and a half acres surrounding the house and barn, and a large open tract across the road. As proof of his success, Edward Dickinson remodeled the Homestead extensively. The red brick exterior received a coat of paint, a pale-yellow ochre. Like a good Victorian, he also added a small conservatory for the cultivation and display of plants.

As a young man Edward Dickinson had planted trees and was especially interested in the kitchen garden. "The strawberries are abundant here," he wrote to Emily Norcross, his future wife,

✿ Emily Dickinson's father, Edward, painted by Otis T. Bullard in the 1840s.

✿ Emily Norcross Dickinson, the poet's mother and namesake.

"& cherries & currants are nearly ripe. The whole vegetable kingdom now appears in its greatest beauty." Later on, he also did some of the legwork for his daughters' garden. "Tell . . . papa to come with the sweet-williams," Emily ordered in 1859.

Emily Norcross Dickinson was also a gardener. Her eldest daughter described her as busy, "with fruit, and plants, and chickens, and sympathizing friends, she really was so hurried she hardly knew what to do." A fine cook and homemaker, she decorated from her flower garden, cutting stems and arranging them in pitchers around the house. She gave her children a love of horticulture. Emily Dickinson once informed her cousin, "I was reared in the garden, you know."

Emily, the middle child, was born in 1830. She followed a year and a half after the firstborn, William Austin. In 1833 Lavinia, the youngest, was born. This trio—Emily, Austin, and Vinnie—shared a passion for plants, a tight-knit relationship, and a lifelong occupancy of the Dickinson property.

Austin, like their father, was a great planter of trees. As a teenager, he planted a grove of white pines near their house. Dickinson reported their progress to her brother, then away at school. "We all went down this morning, and the trees look beautifully," she wrote. "Every one is growing, and when the west wind blows, the pines lift their light leaves and make sweet music." If you stand quietly under

Emily, Austin, and Lavinia Dickinson ages nine, ten, and seven, respectively.

a pine and wait for the wind, the needles—its light leaves—whisper. Susurrate.

Vinnie was her sister's lifelong companion. During Emily Dickinson's reclusive years, Vinnie dealt with the outside world. She was another gardener, described as making borders and training vines. And she wasn't afraid to dig—Emily once referred to her "subsoiling" in the garden. After her sister's death, it was Lavinia Dickinson's discovery of the cache of poems and her persistence in seeing them published that introduced Dickinson to the world.

In an early portrait with her siblings, Emily is nine years old, shown with red hair and a gentle smile. Though the three look stilted in typical period portraiture, the artist painted young Emily Dickinson holding a book and pink rose, the written word and a flower. In the language of flowers, the pink rose symbolized sweetness and innocence, desirable virtues for children of the day. Little did the artist know that Dickinson's voice would endure.

Early Spring in Emily Dickinson's Garden

"There is no more snow!" —From 30, 1858

DAYS ARE LENGTHENING toward the vernal equinox. While an occasional nor'easter still roars up the Atlantic coast, its counter-clockwise arms dumping snow in central New England, it is spring snow and short-lived. Gradually the snows diminish in Emily's garden. She observed one fine March day, "Mother went rambling, and came in with a burdock on her shawl, so we know that the snow has perished from the earth. Noah would have liked mother." (Though the dove from Noah's ark returned with an olive leaf when the floodwaters receded.)

As the ground thaws, the lawn gets greener and bare ground liquifies. Late in the winter of 1857 an editor in the *Amherst Record* described it:

Everything now seems to portent an early spring; not a patch of snow, but everywhere mud, and our friends, the sugar makers in our neighborhood, are improving this season of frosty nights and melting days to gather the luscious maple sap and manufacture the sugar, which needs no puff from our pen to make it go down.

A late winter treat for young Emily was an excursion with friends to a "sugaring off" to see a vat of sap bubbling in a local sugar shack. Fresh maple syrup is a delight of the season.

She called March "that Month of proclamation." In Emily's garden, buds swell on the branches, elbowing into the longer, warmer days. Songbirds charm the trees. Dormant plants, metabolisms slowed during the long Massachusetts winter, wake up. The first flowers to bloom for her each year are the little bulbs.

THE EARLY BULBS, corms, and tubers flower, set seed, and manufacture adequate food stores in late winter and spring, then rest underground, unseen for the remainder of the year.

Glowing is her Bonnet -
Glowing is her Cheek -
Glowing is her Kirtle -
Yet she cannot speak!

Better as the Daisy
From the summer hill
Vanish unrecorded
Save by tearful rill -

Save by loving sunrise
Looking for her face.
Save by feet unnumbered
Pausing at the place.

106B, 1859

Spring Bulbs

Snowdrop (*Galanthus nivalis*). Heralds of spring, the snowdrops lead the way, their nodding, bell-shaped flowers with their own proclamations. Each flower has three inner petals trimmed in green and three outer petals that descend in graceful curves. They are sweet-smelling and long-lived. As a bonus, snowdrops that are happy in their spot increase every year, carpeting an area with white. Sometimes it seems that they are on the move.

❀ Snowdrops multiply and bloom amid "the punctual snow."

New feet within my garden go -
New fingers stir the sod -
A Troubadour opon the Elm
Betrays the solitude.

New Children play opon the green -
New Weary sleep below -
And still the pensive Spring returns -
And still the punctual snow!

79, 1859

Crocus. Dickinson termed the crocus a "vassal" of the snow. A member of the iris family, the crocus has a cup-shaped flower. Tradition dedicates it to St. Valentine since it blooms near his holy day. The 'Cloth of Gold' crocus has been cultivated since the sixteenth century. Other early crocus species that Emily might have grown include the "tommies," *Crocus tommasinianus.* Introduced into the nursery trade in the 1840s, tommies bloom pale to deep lilac with white throats.

Crocuses grow from corms, swollen underground stems crowned by a growing bud. Planted in autumn in well-drained soil, they repay the effort in early spring. The flowers stand up from the frozen ground like straight soldiers. Dickinson also dubbed them "martial." After they bloom, they disappear, leaves and all.

❀ A "martial" crocus salutes the day.

Hyacinth (*Hyacinthus orientalis*). Dense, fragrant hyacinths followed the crocuses. Dickinson remembered a glance from a friend "in Hyacinth time." Gardeners often tell time by the bloom season rather than the calendar. In acknowledgment for a gift of bulbs, she wrote, "The Snow will guide the Hyacinths to where their Mates are sleeping, in Vinnie's sainted Garden." One wonders what conferred sainthood on Lavinia or, at minimum, canonized her garden beds. However, botanically speaking, Emily was accurate. Hyacinth bulbs are among the underground

❀ The flower that bloomed "in Hyacinth time."

🌿 Some of these tulips wear carmine suits.

plant structures with contractile roots. That is, specialized roots pull the bulbs lower in the ground. Whether with a snowy guide or not, is subject to speculation.

Tulip (*Tulipa*). In another of Dickinson's early poems, a sort of schoolgirl puzzle, she described a bulb as asleep and forgotten, save by the gardener. Since the flower in the poem wakes up dressed in carmine and the number of red-flowering spring bulbs is limited, a tulip is the likely subject:

She slept beneath a tree -
Remembered but by me.
I touched her Cradle mute -
She recognized the foot -
Put on her Carmine suit
And see!

15, 1858

Beyond plants of the bulbous tribe, another flower that carpets Emily's garden is the pansy. One she grew was *Viola tricolor*, sometimes called Johnny-jump-ups as they pop up in unlikely places. They can also spread to the dinner table. As pansies are edible, they are lovely additions to salads and superb decorations for ice molds or cakes. When Emily baked gingerbread, she sometimes used them to decorate its shiny surface. Like many flowers of the season, they are diminutive.

A pansy is particular only about the weather. To one friend, Dickinson wrote, "That a pansy is transitive, is its only pang." It will grow in cold weather, languish in hot. She gathered them into spring bouquets and wrote this accompanying poem.

🌱 The pansy, or heart's ease.

I'm the little "Heart's Ease"!
I dont care for pouting skies!
If the Butterfly delay
Can I, therefore, stay away?

If the Coward Bumble Bee
In his chimney corner stay,
I, must resoluter be!
Who'll apologize for me?

Dear - Old fashioned, little flower!
Eden is old fashioned, too!
Birds are antiquated fellows!
Heaven does not change her blue.
Nor will I, the little Heart's Ease -
Ever be induced to do!

167, 1860

The word "pansy" comes from the French word that means "to think." Thus a pansy is pensive, with its flowers that look like faces,

🌿 "I'm the little 'Heart's Ease'!"

faces that invite contemplation. Perhaps that is why another nick-name for this flower is "heart's ease."

As spring moves forward, the earth warms and more perennials emerge, shouldering buds up through the soil. One of the plants in the garden is the peony, masses of peonies. Austin and Susan's daughter, Martha—called Mattie—later remembered "ribbons of peony hedges." A twelve-year-old Emily once compared them to the young rosy face of the stable hand's son. "Tell Vinnie I counted three peony noses, red as Sammie Matthews's, just out of the ground." (Peonies break the soil's surface with pointed burgundy buds that bear a striking resemblance to noses.) Even in adolescence, Emily Dickinson

May 6 . 1899 .
Mrs R.
Hort. Soc.

Borraginaceae
Mertensia . Lungwort
Link.
M. Virginica, DC. Virginian cowslip . L

✗ Virginia bluebells, captured by Massachusetts botanical artist Helen Sharp.

could manage her metaphors. With the ground warming, the little bulbs spent, and the perennials coming into leaf, the stage is set for the peak spring display.

With friends, Emily shared some of her spring's abundance gathered from her garden or further afield. Once she sent pussywillow with an enclosure that read, "Nature's buff message – left for you in Amherst. She had not time to call." Native to wet sunny places in New England, the Upper Midwest, and southern Canada, the pussywillow, *Salix discolor*, is prized for its emerging, fuzzy catkins. It is an energetic small tree or large shrub, depending on one's point of view.

Emily also enclosed pressed flowers in her letters. In a brief note to a fellow poet, she once sent bluebells. "Bluebell" is a common name that graces several plants, including a bulb, English bluebells (*Hyacinthoides non-scripta*), and

꽃 One of Dickinson's friends opened a letter to find this arrangement of pressed pansies. She called them "Satin Cash" in an enclosed poem, a horde of petals paid, as if on account, for many paragraphs.

a spring ephemeral, Virginia bluebells (*Mertensia virginica*). Because the letter is dated early April, it is likely the latter, since English bluebells bloom in Amherst later in spring. Virginia bluebells would have appealed to Dickinson, unfurling fluorescent blue-green leaves in March, nodding with blue clusters of blooms in April, sowing their seed and then disappearing by June. Like her poems, bluebells are startling and succinct.

As the days lengthened, Emily Dickinson took up her trowel, rising earlier, staying out later. She also took up her pen to celebrate the changing cadence.

A Light exists in Spring
Not present on the Year
At any other period -
When March is scarcely here
A Color stands abroad
On Solitary Fields
That Science cannot overtake
But Human Nature feels.

It waits opon the Lawn,
It shows the furthest Tree
Opon the furthest Slope you know
It almost speaks to you.

Then as Horizons step
Or Noons report away
Without the Formula of sound
It passes and we stay -

A quality of loss
Affecting our Content
As Trade had suddenly encroached
Opon a Sacrament -

962, 1865

Early spring is a season of watching.

Late Spring

THE EDUCATION OF A GARDENER

ONE MORNING, Emily's mother received a note from Deborah Fiske, a neighbor across town. Mrs. Fiske wrote, "Professor Fiske will lead Helen over to play with Emily beneath the syringas, this afternoon. In case it prove not convenient to send her home, he will call for her in the chaise before nightfall, before the dew falls." The two girls played under the mock orange, called syringa at the time. There is more significance to this connection between two small girls—both five years old at the time—than a childhood playdate. Helen Fiske would grow up to become Helen Hunt Jackson, an author of note and one of the few people to recognize the genius of the adult Dickinson's poetry. But that would come later.

Did Helen and Emily play in the mud that day in 1836? Emily Elizabeth Dickinson was not a perfect child, receiving the occasional parental scolding. Deportment aside, she had a child's reaction to the natural world—awe and joy— a quality that many lose but she retained. As a little girl, she wandered and came home happy, but bedraggled. Well into adulthood, Dickinson wrote, "I was always attached to Mud."

Young Emily Dickinson in profile, 1845.

She remembered, "two things I have lost with Childhood, the rapture of losing my shoe in the mud and going Home barefoot, wading for Cardinal flowers and the mother's reproof which was more for my sake than her weary own for she frowned with a smile." There was a stream that ran through the Dickinson meadow and others nearby, ready for wading. Deep red cardinal flowers bloomed in moist soils.

After an afternoon of muddy wandering, young Emily might have settled in with the latest issue of *Parley's*, a children's quarterly. Her father bought them for his three offspring. *Parley's* often featured gardening poems, stories, and embellishments—what we call illustrations. "My Dear little Children," Edward wrote, "I send you some of Parley's Magazine—They have some interesting stories for you to read. I want to have you remember some of them to tell me when I get home." An 1839 issue includes a poem called "The Harebell, or Campanula Rotundifolia," by Miss Mary Howitt. Harebells are blue flowers common to Amherst and would be the subject of future Dickinson poems.

For her first nine years, Emily and her family lived in half of the Homestead, sharing the house first with her grandparents, then— after her grandfather's bankruptcy—as tenants with new owners, the Macks. By 1840 with an established law practice, Edward Dickinson could finally afford a home of his own. They moved to a house on North Pleasant Street, a few blocks from where Emily was born. They lived there until 1855.

Everything on the property was demolished decades ago. It was next to the West Cemetery, which is still there. The only surviving photograph shows a comfortable house with a large porch and fruit trees in the front. In May 1842, Emily wrote to Austin, reporting that although the garden hadn't gone in yet—that is, the annual flowers and vegetables hadn't been planted—both grape arbor and lattice work had been painted, and "our trees are all very full of blossoms now and – they look Very handsome."

Their fruit trees were evidently good performers, and there must have been a grape trellis as well. One September, the local paper reported, "Edward Dickinson Esq. of Amherst, sent over a basket

Amherst Academy and Parson House

❧ ABOVE The North Pleasant
Street house where the
Dickinson family lived and
gardened for fourteen years.

❧ LEFT Amherst
Academy, where Emily
first studied botany.

containing a rich variety of fine pears and other fruit . . . Two varieties [of grapes] came in the basket of Edward Dickinson Esq."

Growing up, Emily was a natural storyteller, clever and arch. In a letter to her cousins she described her Aunt Libbie, using the garden as a springboard for family comedy. "The trees stand right up straight when they hear her boots, and will bear crockery wares instead of fruit, I fear." Elizabeth Dickinson Currier must have been a stickler, because her niece concluded, "She hasn't starched the geraniums yet, but will have ample time."

Austin took after his father in his interest in improving the new property. One spring he planted a new sapling near the house. He was concerned with its well-being. "I take good care of the tree," his sister reported in his absence, "give it a pail of water every day, and certainly it looks stouter, and we all think it will live."

While they lived on North Pleasant Street, Emily learned her letters and numbers in the local schoolhouse. She walked there with other children from her neighborhood, kicking through autumn leaves, chasing petals in the spring. On cold winter mornings, a hot potato in her pocket kept her fingers warm. Her parents and grandparents believed in advanced education for all children, boys and girls. Austin went away to boarding school at Williston Seminary in Northampton. When she finished primary school, Emily lived at home and attended Amherst Academy on Amity Street.

Amherst Academy gave Emily Dickinson her first formal lessons about plants. She described her studies enthusiastically to her friend Jane Humphrey. "Besides Latin I study History and Botany I like the school very much indeed." She added, "My Plants grow beautifully."

The school also helped its students to grow with diverse educational opportunities. They attended lectures at Amherst College. Edward Hitchcock, the president of the college, and his colleagues lectured on natural history topics including botany and geology. "We found that the admission of girls to such lectures as they could understand," one writer had documented in 1835, "was a practice of some year's standing, and . . . no evil had been found to result from it."

The Dickinsons and Hitchcocks were in the same social set. Vinnie's best friend was their youngest daughter, Jane. They were companions for walking and shopping, for the reading circle and for parties. Edward Jr. was a lifelong friend of Austin's. In addition to lectures, teaching, and college administration, Doctor Hitchcock preached at Sunday services and wrote books.

"When Flowers annually died, and I was a child," Dickinson recalled, "I used to read Dr Hitchcock's Book on the Flowers of North America. This comforted their Absence – assuring me they lived." An article she had read in the September 1861 issue of *The Atlantic Monthly* entitled "My Out-Door Study" had triggered this childhood memory.

In the essay, the author, Thomas Wentworth Higginson (more about him later) contended that "even the driest and barest book of Natural History is good and nutritious, so far as it goes, if it represents genuine acquaintance; one can find summer in January by poring over the Latin catalogues of Massachusetts plants and animals in Hitchcock's Report." Dickinson reacted to this "summer in January" with her memory of Edward Hitchcock's book. The seasonal cycles of plants—their growth, death, and resurrection—became a frequent trope for Dickinson in her poetry.

Fig. 71. 2d. *Funnel-form*, (*infundibuliformis*, from *infundibulum*, a funnel;) having a tubular base, and a border opening in the form of a funnel, as the Morning-glory, Fig. 71.

3d. *Cup-shaped*, (*Cyathiformis*, from *cyathus*, a drinking-cup;) differing from funnel-shaped, in having its tube, and border, less spreading; and from bell-form, in not having its tube appear as if scooped at out the base, Fig. 72.

Fig. 72.

Fig. 73.

4th. *Salver-form*, (*hypocrateriformis*, from the Greek *kraier*, an ancient drinking glass called a *salver*;) this has a flat, spreading border, proceeding from the top of a tube, Fig. 73.

Fig. 74.

5th. *Wheel-form*, (*rotate*, from *rota*, a wheel;) having a short border without any tube or with a very short one, Fig. 74.

This kind of corolla may be seen in the mullein.

6th. *Labiate*, (from *labia*, lips;) consists of two parts, resembling the lips of a horse, or other animal. Labiate corollas are said to be *personate*,* having the throat closed, or *ringent*,† with the throat open. You have a labiate corolla of the ringent kind, at Fig. 75. The term labiate is also applied to a calyx of two lips. *Bi-labiate* is sometimes used in the same sense as labiate.

Fig. 75.

Different forms of Polypetalous Corollas.

1st. *Cruciform*, (from *crux*, a cross;) consisting of four petals of equal size spreading out in the form of a cross, as the radish, cabbage, &c. Fig. 76.

Fig. 76.

2d. *Caryophyllous*, having five single petals, each terminating in a long claw enclosed in a tubular calyx, as the pink, Fig. 77.

Fig. 77.

3d *Liliaceous*, a corolla with six petals, spreading gradually from the base, so as to exhibit a bell-form appearance, as in the tulip and lily.

4th. *Rosaceous*, a corolla formed of roundish spreading petals without claws, or with very short ones, as the rose and apple.

* From *persona*, a mask.
† From *ringo*, to grin, or gape.

Labiate corollas, how divided ?—Form of polypetalous corollas—Cruciform—Caryophyllous—Liliaceous—Rosaceous.

Funnel-form—Cup-shaped—Salver-form—Wheel-form.

✿ In the edition of *Familiar Lectures on Botany* that Emily used, "corolla" is defined as "that part of the flower which is most remarkable for the liveliness of its colours, the delicacy of its substance, and the sweetness of its perfume."

Amherst Academy introduced Emily to another botanical book. Her science class used Almira Lincoln's textbook *Familiar Lectures on Botany*, a popular book that went through nine editions in ten years. The analysis of plants was considered a genteel occupation for women. If you open the little brown book that Emily opened, the introduction from Mrs. Lincoln reads, "The study of Botany seems peculiarly adapted to females; the objects of its investigation are beautiful and delicate; its pursuit leading to exercise in the open air is conducive to health and cheerfulness."

Emily Dickinson studied many beautiful and delicate flowers in the open air. She practiced her botany in person and in poetry. She described the scientific process:

I pull a flower from the woods -
A monster with a glass
Computes the stamens in a breath -
And has her in a "Class"!

From 117, 1859

Using a magnifying glass she counted the stamens, the pollen-bearing male parts of the flower that entice bird, bee, and botanist. Once counted, the flower could be brought to class, as in classroom, and placed in a class, as in the Linnaean classification system used at the time.

Beyond the taxonomy of plants, Dickinson mined botanical vocabulary. One of Mrs. Lincoln's lectures is entitled "Of the Calyx and Corolla." In Dickinson's poems, both words appear. Blooms open, releasing their scent.

Bright Flowers slit a Calyx
And soared opon a stem
Like Hindered Flags - Sweet hoisted -
With Spices - in the Hem -

From 523, 1863

"Calyx" is the outer covering of the flower. It is made up of scales that protect a flower bud. Thus the calyx is slit when the bud unfurls and the flower is exposed. Of the petals or "corolla" of the fall-blooming fringed blue gentian, she later wrote:

The Gentian has a parched Corolla -
Like Azure dried
'Tis Nature's buoyant juices
Beatified -
Without a vaunt or sheen
As casual as Rain
And as benign -

When most is past - it comes -
Nor isolate it seems -
It's Bond it's Friend -
To fill it's Fringed career
And aid an aged Year
Abundant end -

1458, 1877

In addition to studying botany, Emily began collecting flowers and creating a herbarium, a collection of pressed, dried plants. It was a popular hobby, part of nineteenth-century eclecticism and a continuation of the appetite for science stimulated by the Enlightenment. A fourteen-year-old Emily wrote to her friend Abiah Root:

I have been to walk to-night and got some very choice wild flowers. I wish you had some of them. . . . I am going to send you a little geranium leaf in this letter, which you must press for me. Have you made an herbarium yet? I hope you will if you have not, it would be such a treasure to you; most all the girls are making one.

✿ OPPOSITE The "parched Corolla" of the fringed gentian, from Mrs. Badger's *Wildflowers Drawn and Colored from Nature*.

✿ BELOW A geranium leaf and small cluster of flowers, painted by Orra White Hitchcock, Edward Hitchcock's spouse.

If you do, perhaps I can make some additions to it from flowers growing around here.

She learned about this method of preserving plants in her botany class. "An herbarium neatly arranged is beautiful," wrote Mrs. Lincoln in *Familiar Lectures*, "and may be rendered highly useful, by affording an opportunity to compare many species together, and it likewise serves to fix in the mind the characters of plants." The herbarium was both feminine art and scientific endeavor according to Mrs. Lincoln.

Dickinson's sixty-six-page herbarium is bound in leather with a green fabric cover embossed in a floral pattern. For it, she gathered a flower of more than four hundred plants, often with accompanying stem and leaf. Then she pressed and dried them between sheets of paper or in the pages of large books.

Drying flowers and capturing poems are things that must be done without delay, as Dickinson documented.

I held a Jewel in my fingers -
And went to sleep -
The day was warm, and winds were prosy -
I said "Twill keep" -

I woke - and chid my honest fingers,
The Gem was gone -
And now, an Amethyst remembrance
Is all I own -

261, 1861

Once her specimens were dried, she laid them out on the album's pages. Each specimen was carefully mounted with strips of gummed paper and neatly labeled in her best penmanship.

The layouts are lovely. On many pages Emily offset a single large specimen with several smaller ones. Sometimes the arrangements are whimsical, two daisies crisscrossed at the bottom of a page as if they support a coat of arms. Others are vigorous, three stems of aralia fanned out over a tripartite leaf of hepatica. Later in the album, she inserted more specimens per page, as if she worried about running

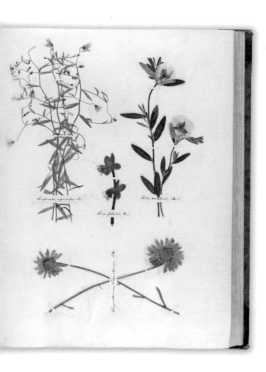

On the eighth page of the herbarium she grouped three wildflowers—marsh bellflower (*Campanula aparinoides*), leatherwood (*Dirca palustris*), and rockrose (*Cistus canadensis*)—and added a flower grown in the garden and the meadow, oxeye daisy (*Chrysanthemum leucanthemum*, now reclassified as *Leucanthemum vulgare*).

out of room. All the pages in the album were used. As she continued to collect specimens, she had to fit them in wherever she found space.

She was catholic in her collecting. Her collection encompassed the flowers of fruits (apple, currant, strawberry), vegetables (potato, tomato, cucumber), and trees (horsechestnut, maple, dogwood) in addition to ornamental plants. She cast a wide net across the natural world, even catching two algae, one freshwater and one from the sea.

As she assembled the pages, Emily experimented with different methods for ordering the diversity. On most pages the genera are mixed. Occasionally she grouped the species of one genus—a page of violas, another of narcissi—leading one to wonder if they were favorites. Seasons mingle. Flowers of lobelia and dogtooth violet bloom on the same page, even though they open months apart. She integrated plants from the garden with plants from the wild.

For a detective in search of Dickinson's garden, the herbarium is dense with clues. The garden flowers that made the cut are hard evidence of what she grew, or at least knew. One of her poems mentions the poppy—her herbarium has both California poppy (*Eschscholzia californica*) and corn poppy (*Papaver rhoeas*). In another poem she announces that "The Lilac is an ancient shrub." The herbarium holds specimens of late-blooming Persian lilac (*Syringa ×persica*) and common lilac (*Syringa vulgaris*). She left us a visual plant list for annuals in her garden beds: zinnias and snapdragons, nasturtiums and four o'clocks.

✿ For this specimen, Dickinson wrote the botanical name for the oxeye daisy, *Chrysanthemum leucanthemum*, and "17-2," for the count of stamens and pistils.

On tiny labels, Emily inked the name of the plant with proper botanical nomenclature: the genus followed by species or specific epithet, following the system devised by Swedish naturalist Carolus Linnaeus (a.k.a. Carl von Linné) a century before her. As instructed in her botany lectures, she counted the stamens and pistils of the flower and wrote numbers below each name to indicate the class and order of the plant.

Mrs. Lincoln suggested an approach to herbarium-making that was a joy for a schoolgirl in a country town: botanical excursions. "You will experience more pleasure from the science, by seeing the flowers in their own homes; a dry grove of woods, the borders of little streams, the meadows, the pastures, and even the way-sides will afford you constant subjects for botanical observations." Botanists call it fieldwork. The Amherst environs offered ample offerings to encourage the botanical interests of Emily and her classmates.

"There were several pleasure parties of which I was a member, and in our rambles we found many and many beautiful children of spring, which I will mention and see if you have found them," she related to Abiah Root, "the trailing arbutus, adder's tongue, yellow violets, liverleaf, blood-root, and many other smaller flowers."

A SELECTION *OF* EMILY DICKINSON'S
Spring Wildflowers

Trailing arbutus (*Epigaea repens*). Emily's "children of spring" include arbutus, a small plant with oval leaves that pushes up through the duff on a woodland floor. Its pink and white flowers bloom from April through May, lending it one of its other common names: mayflower. Rumor has it that mayflower, now the Massachusetts state flower, got its name from the Pilgrims who christened it after their ship. The adult Dickinson used mayflower to pinpoint spring's awakening. Finding the first bloom was an event. When a friend sent arbutus, she called it "a rosy boast." Another spring she wrote, "The mud is very deep – up to the wagons' stomachs – arbutus making pink clothes, and everything alive." In a poem, she described its appearance without revealing its name:

⚘ Trailing arbutus in its "pink clothes," by Clarissa Munger Badger.

Pink - small - and punctual -
Aromatic - low -
Covert in April -
Candid - in May -

Dear to the Moss -
Known of the Knoll -
Next to the Robin
In every Human Soul -

Bold little Beauty -
Bedecked with thee
Nature forswears
Antiquity -

1357, 1875

Adder's tongue (*Erythronium americanum*). Adder's tongue blooms with yellow, lily-shaped flowers, the petals curling back into spirals, and its long, protruding stamens suggesting its reptilian nickname. You might hear it called trout lily because its speckled leaves are similar in coloration to a brook trout. Adder's tongue colonizes shady woodlands, blooming from March through May, depending on the weather. One May day, Dickinson sent a poem to a friend, accompanying a gift of adder's tongue:

Their dappled importunity
Disparage or dismiss -
The Obloquies of Etiquette
Are obsolete to Bliss -

1677, 1885

🌿 Trout lily displaying its "dappled importunity," in a painting by Helen Sharp.

🌿 Dickinson arranged spring-blooming hepatica, then classified as *Hepatica triloba*, with two other wildflowers that bloom across the year: the introduced *Verbascum thapsus* (mullein) blooms in summer and the native *Aralia nudicaulis* (wild sarsaparilla) flowers in early autumn.

Dickinson's poems, including her flower poems, are often opportunities to use the dictionary. "Importunity" means insistent, and May is unseasonably early for lilies. Cultivated lily bulbs all bloom in summer. An "obloquy" is a slander or similar verbal abuse. She implies that bliss beats bad manners. Perhaps Dickinson's floral acknowledgment was belated, or maybe there was a hidden meaning known only to sender and recipient.

Hepatica (*Anemone americana*). Another plant that Emily gathered on her woodland walks was hepatica or American liverleaf. Related to buttercups, species of hepatica grow on both sides of the Atlantic. It has long been used as a medicinal. Native Americans used decoctions of the plant for treatments ranging from digestive and urinary to gynecological. The lobed leaves reminded healers of the shape of the liver. In the formative days of European medicine, the doctrine of signatures suggested that plants that resembled internal organs would prove useful in their treatment. Its charming white flowers are among the first to open in the woods around Amherst.

Bloodroot (*Sanguinaria canadensis*). Like hepatica, bloodroot is another charming wildflower with medical overtones. With its bright red roots, small wonder it was associated with things sanguine— that is, bloody. And indeed it was used for its healing properties. It still appears on lists of homeopathic drugs. In

🌿 Wild bloodroot grows with vigor in the garden beds at the Homestead.

another of Dickinson's botany books, great claims are laid for this small woodland plant, to address a rather terrifying assortment of ills. "Root highly efficacious in the influenza, [w]hooping-cough, and the late epidemic," the author reported, "Also cathartic, emetic and a . . . stimulant." There is no indication that the Dickinsons used these plants as drugs. When Emily Dickinson found liverleaf and bloodroot, she appreciated their properties aesthetic rather than emetic.

As when arranging herbarium specimens, Dickinson sometimes mixed flowers, wild and domestic, in her poetry.

Hush! Epigea wakens!
The Crocus stirs her lids -
Rhodora's cheek is crimson -
She's dreaming of the woods!

Then turning from them reverent -
Their bedtime 'tis, she said -
The Bumble bees will wake them
When April woods are red.

From 85, 1869

The native azalea rhodora (*Rhododendron canadense*) dominates Dickinson's poetic scene. It seems to have been transplanted from the forest to a spot where it blooms alongside garden crocus and *Epigaea*, a wildflower. Still, rhodora yearns for the woods. This plant also inspired Ralph Waldo Emerson to write "The Rhodora, On Being Asked, Whence is the Flower?" in 1834.

The herbarium lets us follow Emily on her wildflower excursions, whispering hints of the habitats she encountered. In addition to a walk in the woods, there is marsh and mud. Waterlilies and marsh marigold, arrowhead and horsetail all like wet feet. You'd have to wade into the tall grass to join her in gathering butterfly weed and goldenrod from the meadow. And some of the plants are postcards from the edge, peering out from the margin of the forest canopy into a clearing. Mountain laurel and elderberry thrive in rich soil and partial shade, making an understory for the woodland trees.

Her siblings shared her plant-collecting pursuits. Vinnie saw it as an opportunity for an outing. "Bowdoin took Mary's French & Lyman,

🌿 Rhodora, "dreaming of the woods!" by Orra White Hitchcock.

E. Fowler & me out to Pelham Springs, last week after Arbutus. We found an abundance of it." And their collecting gave Emily more material for her herbarium, and for financial metaphors. "The Apple Trees lend Vinnie Blossoms which she lends to me, and I pay no interest, their rosy Bank in need of none, and the Woods lend Austin Trilliums, shared in the same way."

Often Emily explored alone. "I had long heard of an Orchis before I found one, when a child, but the first clutch of the stem is as vivid now, as the Bog that bore it," she recalled. An orchis is a hardy terrestrial orchid, one that grows in soil, rather than on trees. Native to New England, they bloom in late spring to early summer. Today, we call them fringed orchids, but these days they appear less frequently in their peaty bogs, showing up instead on endangered plant lists. At close to a foot tall, they are dramatic, especially popping out of a swamp. They appear in both herbarium and poem.

Some Rainbow - coming from the Fair!
Some Vision of the World Cashmere -
I confidently see!
Or else a Peacock's purple Train
Feather by feather - on the plain
Fritters itself away!

The dreamy Butterflies bestir
Lethargic pools resume the whirr
Of last year's sundered tune!
From some old Fortress on the sun
Baronial Bees - march - one by one -
In murmuring platoon!
The Robins stand as thick today
As flakes of snow stood yesterday -
On fence - and Roof - and Twig!
The Orchis binds her feather on
For her old lover - Don the sun!
Revisiting the Bog!
Without Commander! Countless! Still!

The Regiments of Wood and Hill
In bright detachment stand!
Behold, Whose multitudes are these?
The children of whose turbaned seas -
Or what Circassian Land?

162, 1860

Her propensity for solitary wildflower walks did not go unnoticed by her family. In one of Dickinson's letters, you can hear her mother's voice telling her to be careful in a hundred little ways, and her older brother's teasing.

> *When much in the Woods as a little Girl, I was told that the Snake would bite me, that I might pick a poisonous flower, or Goblins kidnap me, but I went along and met no one but Angels, who were far shyer of me, than I could be of them, so I hav'nt the confidence in fraud which many exercise.*

Her father took a different approach to solving the problem of his daughter's solo sojourns. He bought her a really big dog. She named him Carlo, after a canine that appeared in a favorite novel entitled *Reveries of a Bachelor* and called him her "shaggy Ally." Describing her compan-

🌺 The fringed orchis, seen here in a painting by Clarissa Munger Badger, "binds her feather on."

ions to a new correspondent, she listed, "Hills – Sir and the Sundown – and a Dog – large as myself, that my Father bought me – They are better than Beings – because they know – but do not tell."

There is nothing like a dog to take on wildflower walks. "Could'nt Carlo, and you and I walk in the meadows an hour – and nobody care but the Bobolink, and his – a silver scruple?" A well-trained dog is also a proficient gardening supervisor. A dog will lie on the grass soaking up the sun while the gardener digs and toils. A dog will listen, even to the buzz of a hummingbird in the garden.

Within my Garden, rides a Bird
Opon a single Wheel -
Whose spokes a dizzy music make
As 'twere a travelling Mill -

He never stops, but slackens
Above the Ripest Rose -
Partakes without alighting
And praises as he goes,

Till every spice is tasted -
And then his Fairy Gig
Reels in remoter atmospheres -
And I rejoin my Dog,

And He and I, perplex us
If positive, 'twere we -
Or bore the Garden in the Brain
This Curiosity -

But He, the best Logician,
Refers my clumsy eye -
To just vibrating Blossoms!
An Exquisite Reply!

370, 1862

"I talk of all these things with Carlo," Dickinson wrote to a friend, "and his eyes grow meaning, and his shaggy feet keep a slower pace." Evidently, Carlo didn't have the doggish habit of digging holes in the garden with those large shaggy feet or, if he did, she didn't mention it.

Some people say Carlo was a Newfoundland, others that he was a Saint Bernard. But whatever the breed, Carlo was enormous. Emily was pleased with his size. "Vinnie and I are pretty well," she wrote to her sister-in-law who was visiting relatives in New York State. "Carlo – comfortable – terrifying man and beast with renewed activity." In the garden or out, he was a good dog. But he was not Vinnie's favorite.

"Carlo is consistent, has asked nothing to eat or drink, since you went away. Mother thinks him a model dog, and conjectures what he might have been, had not Vinnie 'demoralized' him." Vinnie preferred cats.

Carlo lived a long life, Dickinson's constant companion for sixteen years. One Amherst woman remembered:

> When, as a little girl, she went walking with Miss Dickinson while the huge dog stalked solemnly beside them. "Gracie," said Miss Dickinson, suddenly addressing her child friend, "do you know that I believe that the first to come and greet me when I go to heaven will be this dear, faithful old friend Carlo?"

When he died, Dickinson wrote to a friend, "Carlo died. Would you instruct me now?" After he was gone, she curtailed her excursions. "I explore but little since my mute Confederate, yet the 'infinite Beauty' of which you speak comes too near to seek."

Late Spring in Emily Dickinson's Garden

"The lawn is full of south and the odors tangle, and I hear today for the first the river in the tree."

SPRINGTIME IN AMHERST IS EUPHORIC, a visual and olfactory high. Dickinson called spring an inundation. Bright new leaves pick up the wind, mimicking the sounds of water, its riffles and eddies. The sun heats up flower buds, opening blossoms, drawing out their scent. "Today is very beautiful," Emily once wrote to Austin, "just as bright, just as blue, just as green and as white, and as crimson, as the cherry trees full in bloom, and the half opening peach blossoms, and the grass just waving, and sky and hill and cloud, can make it, if they try."

The fields and yards of Amherst are full of fruit trees. Fruit growing was the common practice among gentlemen farmers, and Edward Dickinson's library included volumes on how to get the best results. In a letter to his future wife, Edward had written, "If we had been married this evening, it would have been as pleasant a time as could have been—I found one of our Peach trees in blossom . . . I always enjoy such pleasant moonlight evenings." Dickinson's father, often

❀ Fruit trees "full in bloom" were a feature of spring in
Amherst. Painting by Clarissa Munger Badger.

portrayed as stern, revealed a streak of romance in this moonlit musing. The flowering orchard must have glowed.

Mattie (her niece) later recalled the fruit trees on the Homestead property. "There were three tall cherry trees in a line, just bordering the flagstone walk at the east side of the house, and all the way down to the garden plum and pear trees, very white and garlandy in spring." Further from the house on a sunny slope, there was an apple orchard started by the patriarch of the family, Samuel Fowler Dickinson.

Orchards then and now are laid out to maximize sun exposure and efficiency, either in squares with trees at four corners or in a pattern of five known as a quincunx. (If you look at dice, the faces with five dots are quincunxes.) Symmetry rules. Underneath the Dickinson orchard, as if protesting this inflicted formality, long grass grows, mingling with wildflowers—violets and buttercups.

The orchard blooms for Dickinson in late spring around Whit Sunday, the seventh Sunday after Easter, known by many as Pentecost. She called the observance "White-Sunday," since it

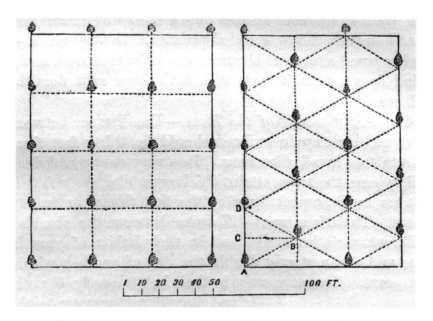

🌾 The Dickinson orchard would have been laid out in a geometric pattern.

coincided with the fruit tree blossoms. When she was old enough to choose, she abstained from the services held in the pillared Congregational church across from Amherst College. She was, as she put it, a dissenter. She practiced her rites in the garden:

Some keep the Sabbath going to Church -
I keep it, staying at Home -
With a Bobolink for a Chorister -
And an Orchard, for a Dome -

Some keep the Sabbath in Surplice -
I, just wear my Wings -
And instead of tolling the Bell, for Church -
Our little Sexton - sings.

"God" preaches, a noted Clergyman -
And the sermon is never long,
So instead of getting to Heaven, at last -
I'm going, all along.

236, 1861

The male bobolink has a clerical coloring. With black plumage, yellow nape, and white scapulars, it looks ready for the choir loft or the pulpit. After the publication of Dickinson's poems in the 1890s, a Boston newspaper reviewer wrote, "Calvinism is a somewhat gnarly tree, but at its core is as sound as eternal righteousness can make it, and the recent graft of liberal thought bears some wonderfully fine olives. This may explain the real reverence which underlies the most startling of Miss Dickinson's utterances."

In late spring gardening activities explode, the time for annual upkeep. In one letter to Austin, his father enumerated the tasks, "The wood is piled—the yard cleaned up—grape vines & trees trimmed—garden made & planted, manure got out, potatoes in lot planted, grass-land dragged over to loosen the earth & make the grass better. The spring business is about over." The ground settles, wrung of its post-winter thaw, and can be worked and amended. Dickinson saved

Primroses edge the spring garden at the Homestead.

"seeds in homes of paper until the sun calls them." These were seeds collected from last year's garden, received from friends, or bought in the shops or from catalogs. It is time to sow.

She knelt down and carefully sowed her seeds, covering them in prepared soil. Her writing immortalized the activity. "I sow my - pageantry in May," she wrote on one page. "It rises train by train." The next poem continues in her spidery handwriting:

> So build the hillocks gaily -
> Thou little spade of mine
> Leaving nooks for Daisy
> And for Columbine -
>
> From 30, 1858

The poem's spade works the soil, raising the levels to allow the planting beds to drain. Planting "nooks" create a loose, natural effect, rather than the tightly patterned carpet bedding popular at the time.

Some seeds can be sowed directly into "nooks" in the prepared soil. Others need to be started under glass and pampered until summer. She documented the process one day, writing, "Vinnie and Sue, are making Hot Beds – but then the Robins plague them so – they don't accomplish much." Unlike a cold frame, a hotbed is heated. It is powered by decomposing manure, giving seeds and seedlings a toasty space to germinate and grow. Emily Dickinson's sister and sister-in-law were getting the hotbeds ready to plant.

Rain signals rest for the gardener, quiet, soft days. "It is lonely without the birds today," Dickinson wrote one wet May day, "for it rains badly, and the little poets have no umbrellas." When the sun comes out, it seems impossibly busy. Emily lavished attention on the garden, kneeling on a red blanket when the ground was damp. Vinnie was there too, writing to her brother, "I feel unusually hurried just now, so many plans suggest themselves for improving the house and grounds."

Late spring is a time to plant the more delicate summer-blooming bulbs like lilies. Dickinson once asked, "Is not an absent friend as mysterious as a bulb in the ground, and is not a bulb the most captivating floral form?" Bulbs and their tuberous kin are a fantastic menagerie. Lily bulbs look like artichokes, dahlias tubers look more like potatoes.

One May, when her friend Cornelia Sweetser sent some bulbs, she responded, "I have long been a Lunatic on Bulbs, though screened by my friends, as Lunacy on any theme is better undivulged." She reported that the bulbs arrived safely and, since planted, "rest in their subterranean Home."

While Dickinson the gardener sowed seeds and planted bulbs for summer flowers, the weeds sowed themselves. Who isn't beset by weeds? Then, as now, dandelions pop up all over lawn and garden. Their serrated leaves conferred the name "dandelion," reminding someone French of lion's teeth or *dent de lion*. The young leaves make a spicy salad or pot green—eating them seems a fitting punishment for the crime of deep taproots that they send into the garden.

Dickinson the writer took a different tack, capturing the dandelion for its images. In various poems, she called the seed heads "shields" and "millinery." In one letter, she pressed a dandelion and tied a

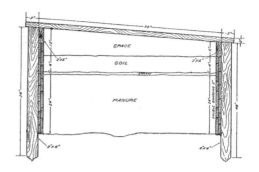

✿ Hotbeds gave the Dickinson sisters a head start on summer.

✿ A red blanket and antique wheelbarrow at the Emily Dickinson Museum along with an original terracotta pot recently discovered at The Evergreens.

✿ Who wouldn't be a lunatic about a bulb like this lily?

ribbon around it, enclosing it with a poem. It is a poetic celebration, an ecstatic paean to spring.

The Dandelion's pallid Tube
Astonishes the Grass -
And Winter instantly becomes
An infinite Alas -
The Tube uplifts a signal Bud
And then a shouting Flower -
The proclamation of the Suns
That sepulture is o'er -

1565, 1882

May Day is the first of May, a day when the Dickinson siblings gathered flowers from the garden to put in May baskets, small containers hung on doors from ribbon handles. Austin, while courting, was known to leave one for a sweetheart on occasion. Bleeding heart grows in their spring garden. Forget-me-nots also flower there. Dickinson once enclosed some of their petite blue and yellow blooms with this advice, "I send you a little Antidote to the love of others – Whenever you feel yourselves enticed, cling to it's Admonition."

🌿 The "pallid Tube" of the dandelion.

🌿 OPPOSITE One of the "'shares' in Primrose 'Banks," as painted by Orra White Hitchcock.

At times Dickinson tallied her spring garden like some Dickensian miser, though as we have seen, she was generous in sharing its dividends.

Then I have "shares" in Primrose "Banks" -
Daffodil Dowries - spicy "stocks" -
Dominions - broad as Dew -
Bags of Doubloons - adventurous Bees
Brought me - from firmamental seas -
And Purple - from Peru -

From 266, 1861

With banks that multiplied each year, the garden's poetic sum was rich in floral prosperity.

The garden is lush with scent. Carpets of lily-of-the-valley, or "vale lily" as she called it, are redolent. The women of the family gathered it for the house and to adorn family graves. The lilacs in the garden are laden with panicles, heavy with perfume. Dickinson described them as delusive, reminding her "Of idleness and Spring." They are long-lived.

The Lilac is an ancient Shrub
But ancienter than that
The Firmamental Lilac
Opon the Hill tonight -
The Sun subsiding on his Course
Bequeaths this final plant
To Contemplation - not to Touch -
The Flower of Occident.

Of one Corolla is the West -
The Calyx is the Earth -
The Capsules burnished Seeds the Stars -
The Scientist of Faith
His research has but just begun -
Above his Synthesis
The Flora unimpeachable
To Time's Analysis -
"Eye hath not seen" may possibly
Be current with the Blind
But let not Revelation
By Theses be detained -

1261, 1872

Lilacs attract never-idle bees. In one letter, Dickinson wrote, "I must just show you a Bee, that is eating a Lilac at the Window. There – there – he is gone! How glad his family will be to see him!" The worker bee (a "she" rather than "he," as all worker bees are female) is

🐝 Lilacs ready to bloom on ancient shrubs behind the Homestead.

gathering nectar and pollen for the hive—nectar for honey, pollen for
the apian equivalent of bread, stored to feed bee brood.

I wonder if Emily Dickinson knew that bees make bread, as she
was the family's baker. She was fond of bees as an ever-ready source
of inspiration and onomatopoeia, her "Buccaneers of Buzz." They
pirate from her spring garden, building their stores for summer. And
while they travel, they never forget home.

Early Summer

A GARDENER'S TRAVELS

AS MUCH AS A GARDENER LOVES A PATCH OF GROUND—her own cir-
cumference—travel is tempting. Other landscapes, other gardens,
offer comparison and stimulation. Travel can be a gardener's muse, as
well as a poet's.

In her teens and early twenties, Emily Dickinson traveled
often. She visited relatives around Massachusetts, and Boston was
a special draw. In 1846, she spent a month there, staying with her
Aunt Lavinia and Uncle Loring Norcross. She played the tourist.
"I have been to Mount Auburn, to the Chinese Museum, to Bunker
Hill," she recounted to Abiah Root. "I have attended 2 concerts & 1
Horticultural exhibition. I have been upon the top of the State house &
almost everywhere that you can imagine."

The horticultural exhibition! Aunt Lavinia took Emily to the
Saturday display of fruits, flowers, and vegetables at the rooms of
the Massachusetts Horticultural Society. The society, that venerable
institution, was relatively new at the time, founded in 1829. It ran one
of the first flower shows in America, and it continues to run competi-
tions, public programs, and a research and lending library dedicated
to the plant world. On September 16, 1846, the society commenced its
"Eighteenth Annual Exhibition of Fruits, Flowers, Floral Decorations
and Vegetables," with opening hours on Tuesdays, Wednesdays, and
Thursdays. It was this event that Emily Dickinson attended.

The cut-flower entries Dickinson saw at the September show
featured late-season blooms: asters and fall-blooming roses, annuals

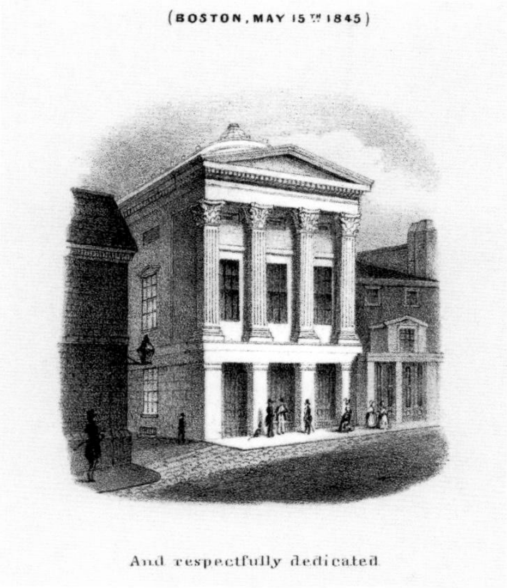
(BOSTON, MAY 15TH 1845)
And respectfully dedicated

Horticultural Hall at 40 School Street in Boston where Emily Dickinson attended the 1846 exhibition.

like amaranth, cockscomb, abutilon, and dahlias. Over the years, Dickinson added some of these plants to her own garden—she mentioned asters and amaranth in later letters.

The spectacular show gardens at the exhibition displayed Victorian eclecticism at its best. Dickinson and her relations were treated to full-scale versions of a Grecian floral temple, a Swiss cottage decorated with moss and flowers, and a pagoda complete with a Chinese tea merchant and finished with fuchsias. There was a salute to the English picturesque in the form of a fourteen-foot Gothic-revival folly framed with evergreens. This round-the-world promenade demonstrated the skill of the designers as well as their wide-ranging taste. It gives a glimpse of what the American garden cognoscenti were up to at the time.

There were huge arrangements in vases and urns, wreaths and garlands hung from walls and ceilings, and flat designs. One that Dickinson would have seen was "a beautiful flat fancy design of large dimensions, presenting a surface wrought with asters, amaranths, and other flowers, with the words 'Horticultural Exhibition, 1846,' inscribed in a border around it, wrought with immortal flowers: on the top of the design was an eagle composed of flowers." Flat designs were the cut-floral equivalent of pattern bedding, that nineteenth-century propensity to make designs in flowers beds. They sound like the floats in a twenty-first-century Tournament of Roses Parade.

There was healthy rivalry in the Exhibition's fruit classes. Growers entered their apples, peaches, plums, figs, and grapes, but most of all they brought their pears. One horticulturist displayed 176 varieties. Their descriptive names—Belle et Bonne, Green Sugar,

Miel de Waterloo, to name a few—had a poetry of their own. The Dickinsons, too, were avid fruit growers. While they seem to have only entered local Amherst shows, they shared the competitive spirit of submitting their produce for judging.

Aunt Lavinia Norcross, a frequent visitor to the Boston exhibitions, once wrote to Emily's mother, "I attended the Horticultural Exhibition last eve . . . It reminds us of the garden of Eden—Such a profusion of splendid flowers & such fruit—but every now & then was a slip of paper & on it written 'Touch Not.'" Did Aunt Lavinia or Emily succumb to temptation and touch any of the forbidden fruit on their sojourn at Horticultural Hall?

The writer Emily Dickinson did not resist the original garden and its forbidden fruit. Its elements are rich: Adam and Eve, plants and animals in abundance, and sin in the guise of a slithering snake proffering a divine apple. Genesis as biblical allusion garners a Congregationalist seal of approval yet remains faintly risqué—life in the garden before the fig leaf. Dickinson often employed Eden, once writing, "Expulsion from Eden grows indistinct in the presence of flowers so blissful, and with no disrespect to Genesis, Paradise remains."

Speaking of Paradise, Emily Dickinson's destinations for her 1846 Boston trip also included Mount Auburn Cemetery. To present-day sensibilities, it may seem unusual to add a cemetery to a sightseeing itinerary, but not in her day. She and her relations might have taken the new omnibus, a horse-drawn trolley launched in 1845 to take some of the thousands of visitors from downtown Boston directly to Cambridge.

They would have come in via the north entrance on Mount Auburn Street, through a huge granite Egyptian gate, like entering some ancient temple along the Nile. The grounds—nearly 175 acres—were sculpted around ancient black oaks and planted with ornamental trees and shrubbery. Emily and her relations meandered along curving roads, new scenes revealed at each turn. Streets were most often named for plants: Oak Avenue and Hibiscus Path, their names embossed on cast iron signs.

Horses were not allowed, so the Norcross-Dickinson party walked, looking across ponds that reflected appropriately weeping willows, and up to the crest of Mount Auburn for the view of the Charles River

🌿 An 1848 etching of Mount Auburn Cemetery, the "City of the dead" that Emily Dickinson described.

and Boston beyond. The graves themselves often were marked with elegant carved memorials and iron fences. Yet they blended with the landscape, rather than dominating it, as if upon returning to dust, individual identities merged back into nature. It was picturesque, irregular, and interesting.

Dickinson shared her impressions in a letter to a friend, writing:

> *Have you ever been to Mount Auburn? If not you can form but slight conception – of the "City of the dead." It seems as if Nature had formed the spot with a distinct idea in view of its being a resting place for her children, where wearied & dissapointed [sic] they might stretch themselves beneath the spreading cypress & close their eyes "calmly as to a nights repose or flowers at set of sun."*

Mount Auburn Cemetery was celebrating its fifteenth anniversary when Dickinson visited. Laid out in 1831 under the aegis of the Massachusetts Horticultural Society, Mount Auburn was the first, and is arguably the most famous, garden cemetery in America. In the days of colony and early statehood, burial grounds were usually dismal, weedy sites crowded with headstones and hemmed into churchyards. By the nineteenth century, forward-thinking planners conceived of turning cemeteries into naturalistic, romantic landscapes. A rural cemetery perfectly suited an emerging romantic sensibility like Emily Dickinson's.

Mount Auburn and its imitators—Laurel Hill in Philadelphia and Green-Wood in Brooklyn to name just two—became major tourist draws. People in cities had few manicured public spaces until the urban park movement emerged some decades later. Families would pack picnics and take them to the cemetery. Couples courted. School classes visited the graves of the famous, ready to be inspired by deeds of the deceased. Horticultural enthusiasts would monitor the plantings, a botanical garden for the dead and their visitors.

But, like any good gardener, Emily worried about her own garden while she was away. Was it adequately watered? What bloom was she missing? "Do you have any flowers in Norwich?" she asked Abiah, "My garden looked finely when I left home. It is in . . . [Vinnie's] care during my absence." She had solved the gardener's dilemma by delegating maintenance to her baby sister.

The same was likely true when she set off for Mount Holyoke Female Seminary the following year, in September 1847. Later renamed Mount Holyoke College, this was where Dickinson would spend her longest time away from home. She was almost seventeen years old. Trunk packed and loaded into the carriage, they pulled out of Amherst. The horses' hooves clicked a reassuring rhythm all the way to South Hadley. They passed familiar sights—farms and mills—and rattled through the covered bridge that crossed the Fort

✻ Lavinia Dickinson took care of the garden when her sister was away.

MOUNT HOLYOKE SEMINARY.
SOUTH HADLEY, MASS.

When Dickinson attended in 1847, the college was
called Mount Holyoke Female Seminary.

River. As they pulled up to the large white building that housed the seminary, it must have seemed strange and remote, though it was only ten miles away.

She roomed in the upstairs dormitory with her cousin Emily Norcross. (The family's propensity for reusing names makes the family tree confusing.) Their room, simply furnished and lit with whale-oil lamps, was too cold for houseplants, even with a Franklin stove. "How do the plants look now & are they flourishing as before I went away?" she asked Austin in November. "I wish much to see them. Some of the girls here, have plants, but it is a cold place & I am very glad that I did not bring any, as I thought of doing."

Dickinson attended classes in science and the classics. She continued her plant studies as documented in this poem.

If the foolish, call them "flowers" -
Need the wiser, tell?
If the Savans "Classify" them
It is just as well!

The stanza might be an anthem for twenty-first-century gardeners who bemoan changes to familiar botanical names. Revisions to taxonomy and nomenclature have accelerated since genetics—called systematics for botany—came onto the scene. For Dickinson, the savants "Classify." If she were revising her poem at present, she might substitute "Reclassify," as scientists realign plant genera into new families based on DNA analysis.

Dickinson's poem continues from flowers, encompassing subjects from the theological to other arenas of the scientific:

Those who read the "Revelations"
Must not criticize
Those who read the same Edition -
With beclouded Eyes!

Could we stand with that Old "Moses" -
"Canaan" denied -
Scan like him, the stately landscape
On the other side -

Doubtless, we should deem superfluous
Many Sciences,
Not pursued by learned Angels
In scholastic skies!

Low amid that glad Belles lettres
Grant that we may stand -
Stars, amid profound Galaxies -
At that grand "Right hand"!

179, 1860

Emily Dickinson had a wide reach.

To acquire her *belle-lettres*, Dickinson followed the rigorous Mount Holyoke schedule. It reads like a military school's. "At 6 o'clock, we all rise. We breakfast at 7. Our study hours begin at 8," she recited in a letter home. "At 9 we all meet in Seminary Hall for devotions." Classes and music practice were held before and after dinner, the main meal of the day, served at 12:30. "At 4½ [4:30] we . . . receive advice from Miss Lyon in the form of a lecture. We have Supper at 6 and silent study hours from then until the retiring bell, which rings at 8¾." Sometime in this daily drill they squeezed in calisthenics and a one-mile walk.

She left school and returned home in August 1848, telling a friend that her father had decided not to send her back. It wasn't unusual. Of her class of 115, only 23 returned for a second year. Seldom did women attend college in those days, and even fewer finished a full degree program.

IN 1853, MR. DICKINSON went to Washington as a newly elected United States congressman, providing the opportunity for a major excursion. The Honorable Edward Dickinson's letters home speak of the House of Representatives, as well as the weather in the District—sirocco winds in summer, and early spring when the "trees show their green, a little, & the grass in the Capitol grounds is the greenest that I ever saw." His wife and two daughters arrived in the middle of February 1855.

During their three weeks in the city, they stayed at Willard's Hotel. It must have been unseasonably warm that year. Emily Dickinson described the weather as "sweet and soft as summer . . . maple trees in bloom and grass green in sunny places." She seemed most impressed with Mount Vernon, recording:

> One soft spring day we glided down the Potomac in a painted boat, and jumped upon the shore – how hand in hand we strode along up a tangled pathway till we reached the tomb of General George Washington, how we paused beside it, and no one spoke a word, then hand in hand, walked on again, not less wise or sad for that marble story; how we went within the door – raised the latch he lifted when he last went home . . . Oh, I could spend a long day, if it did not weary you, telling of Mount Vernon!

In lyrical prose, Dickinson is describing a popular spot, the romance of the graves of the great once again in the fore. If she *had*

WASHINGTONS TOMB.

🌿 An image of George Washington's tomb at Mount Vernon
that is as romanticized as Dickinson's description of it.

spent the long day telling of Mount Vernon, she would have told of the broad porch looking east across the river to the sweep of the Maryland shore. The white clapboard house with its open arcaded arms stretched over the high point of the property, affording it the best view.

Was her description of Mount Vernon written with an ironic twist? It would have been in embarrassing disrepair. Washington's descendants were running low on funds. That July, they sold the estate. The Mount Vernon Ladies Association's preservation efforts did not start until the end of the decade. Still, Emily Dickinson might have walked under some of his specimen trees on that February day and seen the remains of the walled ornamental garden and the kitchen garden. The orangery was there, that elegant brick and glass structure General Washington built to house his tender plants.

At one point during their stay in the nation's capital, Austin sent a teasing letter from home. In a subsequent response, Emily was having none of it. "He says we forget 'the Horse, the Cats, and the geraniums' . . . proposes to sell the farm and move west with mother – to make bouquets of my plants, and send them to his friends." But, she countered, "as for my sweet flowers, I shall know each leaf and every bud that bursts, while I am from home." With Congress adjourned, the Dickinsons returned to Amherst and Austin by way of Philadelphia. Their garden awaited.

❧ The Dickinson family in silhouette at about the time Edward Dickinson was in Congress.

Early Summer in Emily Dickinson's Garden

> You know who "June" is -
> I'd give her -
> Roses a day from Zinzebar -
> And Lily tubes - like wells -
> Bees - by the furlong -
> Straits of Blue -
> Navies of Butterflies - sailed thro' -
> And dappled Cowslip Dells -
> —From 266, 1861

AMONG THE SWEET FLOWERS that Dickinson knew so well were peonies and irises. Peonies nod their languorous heads. Ants march steadily on the unopened buds, like suitors for debutantes, attracted by the nectar. If there has been a heavy rain, there is havoc in the peony hedge. Water weights the blooms, pulling down stems. The bluish-gray sword leaves of the iris contrast in texture and shape. The blooms each last a day, breathless compared to the peony progression.

Roses are the dominant note in the Dickinson flower garden in early summer. Climbers bloom on the two arbors and over a summer house. Great arched canes of old-fashioned shrub roses stretch out into the path, covered with blossoms. Mattie inventoried the varieties in the garden that she remembered:

> *The tiny Greville rose with its clustering buds, each stem a complete little bouquet in itself, my grandmother had brought with her from Monson when she came to Amherst as a bride in 1828; and it is still cherished in our garden today. Beside the yellow and white rose bushes there were long hedges of Hedge-hog roses—named for their ferocious thorns,—and a blur of confusion where the Blush roses spread every year on all sides, as well as a variety of single rose they called the Cinnamon rose— renamed by our generation Love-for-a-day roses because they flare and fall between sunrise and sunset. Among these was a variegated crimson and white striped rose they called the Calico rose, from its likeness to gay chintz . . . This is also blooming yet in our garden, flouting attempts by successive florists at repro-duction. More than one June slips have been given gladly, but the dear old loyalists would never be vulgarized by any such lure of modern publicity.*

To last through cold New England winters, roses in the Dickinson garden needed to be hardy, but there were many varieties that fit the bill. Today, our rose sensibilities have narrowed to either a florist's definition—roses that are long stemmed, usually red, with fat blooms, little scent, and sold by the dozen—or roses that are hardy enough for parking lots like the ubiquitous 'Knockout' series. But the genus *Rosa* has a big family tree. The species that grew in Dickinson's garden are worth seeking out.

ONE SUMMER DAY, Emily Dickinson sent some roses to her friend Emily Fowler. "I quite forgot to mention the *Rosebugs* when I spoke of the buds, last evening, and I found a family of them taking an early breakfast on my most precious bud, with a smart little worm for Landlady, so the sweetest are gone, but accept my love with the smallest." Roses are subject to a bestiary of bugs during the growing

Roses

Damask rose (*Rosa damascena*). Dickinson described this rose in a poem as her "damask maid." These modest, three-inch roses open in clusters of flattened rosettes. The shoots are thorny, "an ambuscade" especially for the gardener trying to clip some blooms. They are an ancient class of roses, cultivated for centuries in the Middle East (*damascena* is for Damascus), by Romans during the Empire, and by the French as far back as the tenth century. The flowers subdue the bees with their fragrance.

Greville rose (*Rosa multiflora* 'Grevillei'). If you read the *Household Cyclopedia of General Information*, published in 1881, you'll find a reference to the Greville rose. Bred in 1816, it was a popular climber from then on. The large double flowers open in luxurious trusses, and their color may stop visitors in their tracks. In a single cluster, blooms range from pale pink to magenta. Aficionados thought that there were seven shades of pink and dubbed the plant the "Seven Sisters" rose. (Note that this is a close relative of the multiflora rose, invasive in much of the United States. Check with your local agricultural extension service before planting.)

Hedgehog rose (*Rosa rugosa*). A hedgehog is a small, spiny European mammal. We call a similar North American animal a porcupine. The hedgehog rose is equally prickly. While native to northern China, the Korean peninsula, and the archipelago of Japan, it has naturalized across the New England dunes, suggesting its other moniker, the salt spray rose. Its botanical epithet, *rugosa*, describes the wrinkled—technically "rugose"—look of its glossy green leaves. For those of you who don't have the time or inclination to fuss with a rose, the rugosa is for you. It will reward you with fragrant single flowers: white, pink, yellow, or purple, depending on the cultivar. And in the fall, the rose hips that remain after the petals fall will turn bright red.

✿ Roses painted by Orra White Hitchcock.

Blush rose (*Rosa* 'Blush Noisette'). A new introduction in Dickinson's day, the blush rose is an American variety from nineteenth-century South Carolina. A Charleston horticulturist named Philippe Noisette bred the hybrid. The 'Blush Noisette' in the Dickinson garden had pale-pink, lightly scented blooms. Unlike many older favorites that flower only in June, the Noisettes are known for their repeat bloom, providing interest until frost.

Rosa gallica 'Versicolor' is the striped calico rose.

❀ The "Love-for-a-Day" or cinnamon rose.

Cinnamon rose (*Rosa majalis*). Nurserymen introduced the cinnamon rose into the trade sometime before 1600. They thought the flower exuded the scent of cinnamon, a prized culinary spice, and the petals and hips of this rose were also consumed by the seventeenth-century equivalent of foodies. There is no indication that the Dickinsons had a taste for this rose in any way other than for its ornamental value. With single pink flowers of spicy scent in June and orange-red hips in the fall garden, it is ornamental indeed.

Calico rose (*Rosa gallica*). While the calico rose might seem suitable for a fabric design, its name is a corruption of its botanical epithet, *gallica*. "Gallica" morphed into "calico," perhaps because of its propensity toward pattern. A number of cultivars of *R. gallica* have variegated petals, striped with pink, white, and magenta, such as the one that Mattie described.

Sweetbrier rose (*Rosa eglanteria*). In Shakespeare's *A Midsummer Night's Dream*, Titania is lulled to sleep under a canopy of eglantine, another name for sweetbrier. Just as Dickinson read Shakespeare, she also grew what she called "mother's sweetbrier." Perhaps this rose with its single pink flowers was one of the plants that Emily Norcross Dickinson had brought with her to Amherst when she married Edward. It grows into a massive shrub. Sweetbrier leaves when bruised exude a fragrance like sliced apples. In autumn, like so many species roses, it puts on a show of ruby hips.

❀ LEFT A floriferous branch of sweetbrier painted by Clarissa Munger Badger.

season. Her rosebugs might have been midges or aphids, but they were most likely one of the species of rose slug. Biologically neither worms nor slugs, they are the larval stages of the sawfly, a primitive wasp, with ravenous appetite for rose leaves and buds.

Roses were one of Emily Dickinson's favorite flowers, based on their frequency in her letters and poems. Always alert to a clever turn of phrase, she wrote to one correspondent, "Vinnie picked the *Sub rosas* in your note and handed them to me." In one letter that she sent, a dried rosebud is hand stitched onto the page. This poem omits the word "rose," a riddle for the recipient.

Pigmy seraphs - gone astray -
Velvet people from Vevay -
Belles from some lost summer day,
Bees exclusive Coterie -

Paris could not lay the fold
Belted down with emerald -
Venice could not show a cheek
Of a tint so lustrous meek -
Never such an ambuscade
As of brier and leaf displayed
For my little damask maid -

I had rather wear her grace
Than an Earl's distinguished face -
I had rather dwell like her
Than be "Duke of Exeter" -
Royalty enough for me
To subdue the Bumblebee.

96, 1859

This poem is Dickinson's substitute Grand Tour, complete with imagined meetings, hospitable hosts, and continental capitals and resorts. For Dickinson, actual travel to Boston, Washington, and

Philadelphia or poetic forays to Paris, Venice, or Great Britain didn't overshadow a stroll among her Amherst roses. When she and her family moved across town, back to the old mansion on Main Street that her grandfather built, wallpaper patterned with roses would cover her bedroom walls.

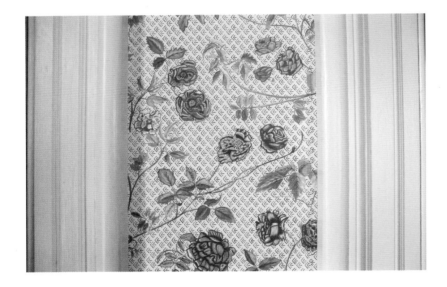

Emily Dickinson's bedroom wallpaper, restored from a fragment discovered during a recent renovation.

Midsummer

A GARDENER'S GROUND

☙

IN 1854 THE ORIGINAL HOMESTEAD on Main Street came on the market. Edward Dickinson, now established in his law practice as well as politics, grabbed the chance. He was buying back the house his father had lost, reasserting his birthright through a real estate transaction. Samuel Fowler Dickinson's ghost was assuaged.

Emily's father reacquired the brick house, outbuildings, ample property around the house, and the eleven-plus acre meadow across the street. He sank a substantial amount into renovations, hiring contractors to add fashionable Italianate features: a cupola, marble mantels for the fireplaces, architraves over the windows in the paired parlors, French doors and the piazza on the west side, a small plant conservatory on the east side in the corner between the study and the dining room. It took the better part of a year for the carpenters and masons to finish their work.

When the projects were complete, the family uprooted themselves from home and garden on Pleasant Street and moved back to the Homestead. Dickinson mused:

> *I supposed we were going to make a "transit," as heavenly bodies did – but we came budget by budget, as our fellows do, till we fulfilled the pantomime contained in the word "moved." It is a kind of gone-to-Kansas feeling, and if I sat in a long wagon, with my family tied behind, I should suppose without doubt I was a party of emigrants!*

🪶 The Homestead's cupola, the apex of Edward Dickinson's 1854–55 renovations, lent an elevated view of the landscape.

🪶 BELOW The Dickinson home on Main Street after the renovations.

At the front door, a silver doorplate welcomed these short-distance émigrés.

It took her some time to get used to living there again. "They say that 'home is where the heart is,'" she wrote. "I think it is where the *house* is, and the adjacent buildings." But she soon discovered or rediscovered her preferred nook. She dubbed a hallway linking the kitchen with the formal front rooms "the Northwest passage," an elusive but profitable channel. It was one of her favorite retreats, with five exits that included a back

RESIDENCE OF HON. EDWARD DICKINSON.

stairway and a door to the outside. A friend of the family remembered calling on Dickinson:

> She received me in a little back hall that connected with the kitchen. It was dimly lighted. She asked if I would have a glass of wine or a rose. I told her I would take the rose, and she went to the garden and brought one in to me. She seemed very unusual, and her voice, her looks, and her whole personality made an impression on me that is still very vivid after all these years.

Home may be where the house is and, for Emily Dickinson, definitely where the garden is. She was soon picking quantities of flowers from the Homestead's flowerbeds. In these years, she still enjoyed making social calls around town, leaving her embossed calling card and sometimes a bouquet. Since there was reserved seating on Sundays at the First Parish Meeting House of the Amherst Congregational Church, on occasion she would deposit bouquets for friends in their family pews before a service.

Dickinson called her bouquets "nosegays." She would make them of a variety of flowers, pressed together in concentric circles, then taped or tied to hold them in place. She got creative. "On one occasion a friend received a more formal and more elaborate bouquet than usual, with a line of admonition in regard to one flower. Upon examination, and the removal of the flower, a tiny note was found wound around the stem, carefully concealed from view."

She was writing more than little notes to hide in nosegays. This was a productive period for Dickinson the poet. She sat at one of two small square cherry writing desks, one in her father's study looking out onto the

🌿 A bouquet like the ones Emily Dickinson assembled and delivered.

conservatory and the other in her bedroom. From her front bedroom windows—their orientation, their altitude—she could ponder the view. Past the bucolic Dickinson meadow, there were the railroad tracks, the smokestack of the hat factory—busy manufacturing hats

🌿 A detail from an 1886 map of Amherst shows the Homestead on Main Street as well as the hat factory and railroad tracks to the south beyond the Dickinson meadow.

out of imported palm leaf—and beyond, the Holyoke Range. Progress hemmed in by permanence. Leaning out and looking east, the green waves of the Pelham Hills rolled toward her.

Dipping her pen in a dark inkwell, she wrote words. A word, say the name of a flower like "rose," became a construct—part memory, part imagination. Imbedded in a poem, with meter and rhyme, words became like the petals of a rose, each different but creating a rhythm and a symmetry.

She was both writer and reader, and among her readings were selections about gardens, flowers, and nature. During Emily Dickinson's life, garden writing flourished as new technology fueled printing, and gardening became America's pastime for both men

🌿 The Dickinsons had an extensive library.

and women. She read Thoreau and Emerson, those bards of eastern Massachusetts, and shared their propensity for transcending humdrum life by focusing on nature. George Eliot and Elizabeth Barrett Browning were favorites. She read articles about flowers, gardens, and the natural world in magazines like *The Atlantic Monthly*—the Dickinsons subscribed. A gardener who reads never gardens alone.

Her father brought her a book when she was twenty-eight years old, *Wildflowers Drawn and Colored from Nature*. He inscribed it "To my daughter Emily from her father Edw. Dickinson January 1, 1859." It was large folio with sentimental poems and rich chromolithographs of flowers and leaves. With its gold-embossed cover and subject matter, it must have made a lovely companion to Emily's herbarium. A botanical artist from Connecticut, Clarissa Munger Badger was the artist-author. I like to think that Edward Dickinson meant to encourage his daughter with this example of a New England woman in print.

After moving back to the house on Main Street, Dickinson's traveling days mostly came to an end. She settled back into the home of

❧ The wildflower book by Clarissa Munger Badger is open on the table in the Homestead study.

her birth and worked on making her garden and her poetry, though
this poem alludes to the Greek island of Paros, known for its white
"Parian" marble:

It will be Summer - eventually.
Ladies - with parasols -
Sauntering Gentlemen - with Canes -
And little Girls - with Dolls -

Will tint the pallid landscape -
As 'twere a bright Boquet -
Tho' drifted deep, in Parian -
The Village lies - today -

The Lilacs - bending many a year -
Will sway with purple load -
The Bees - will not despise the tune -
Their Forefathers - have hummed -

The Wild Rose - redden in the Bog -
The Aster - on the Hill
Her everlasting fashion - set -
And Covenant Gentians - frill -

Till Summer folds her miracle -
As Women - do - their Gown -
Or Priests - adjust the Symbols -
When Sacrament - is done -

374, 1862

Midsummer in Emily Dickinson's Garden

"My Art, a Summer Day"—From 553, 1863

IMAGINE A MELLOW EVENING IN JUNE, the French doors in the Dickinson parlor flung open, their panes reflecting the trees and lawn in the rippling of Victorian-era glass. The faint sound of a piano drifts over from a neighbor's parlor. It is undeniably summer.

After supper, the sun is still high enough to light the interior of the double parlor, cutting an angled swath on the wooden floorboards. Dust motes hang in the air even though spring cleaning was just finished. The windows shine. The carpets have been beaten and rolled up for the summer. Blankets are airing outdoors. Summarizing her attitude toward housework, the always-succinct Dickinson once said, "I prefer pestilence." She preferred gardening.

Stepping through the French doors onto the piazza, you find yourself among potted plants. The oleanders in their green tubs have been lugged out from the conservatory, their thin shiny leaves building energy for a late August bloom. They are joined by the daphne that had bloomed under glass over the winter and now sets new buds in the long summer days.

Summer was Emily Dickinson's favorite season. She mentions it more than any other—there are 145 references to summer in her poems. Its closest competitor, winter, tallies a mere 39. Summer reaches out to her from the garden. On the garden path, one is caught in its tidal pull.

> My Garden - like the Beach -
> Denotes there be - a Sea -
> That's Summer -
> Such as These - the Pearls
> She fetches - such as Me
>
> 469, 1862

With the trees leafed out, pools of shade move clockwise through each day. Leaves riffle like river water moving over rocks in a slow current. Having lost their spring fluorescence, they darken with a concentration of chlorophyll. The subtle oak flowers, its male catkins flinging dusty pollen on the flagstones.

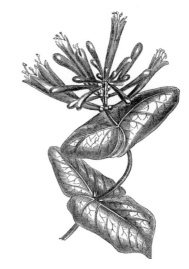

Honeysuckle twines up a trellis just outside the library, its scent taking over where the lilacs left off. The nectar in the tubular pink flowers summons a hummingbird. It hovers above a target bloom and sticks in a long cake-tester tongue to sample the sweetness.

New vines need to be coaxed and tied onto their supports, a snake charmer's art. Emily sometimes took on the job. "I went out before tea tonight, and trained the Honeysuckle," she once reported, "it grows very fast and finely." She added that both plants were covered

🌿 "Honeysuckle – it grows very fast and finely."

in buds. Other times her sister took on the task. "Vinnie trains the Honeysuckle – and the Robins steal the string for Nests – quite, quite as they used to," Dickinson reported.

It is a lovely evening for a walk in the garden—a perambulation if you like. The long twilight near the solstice seems suited to nobility. Purple irises glow.

> Morning - is the place for Dew -
> Corn - is made at Noon -
> After dinner light - for flowers -
> Dukes - for setting sun!
>
> 223, 1861

If the leaves in the iris bed seem to be moving faster than the breeze, it is probably one of Vinnie's cats stalking a small rodent among the rhizomes. Lavinia loved her cats and christened them with silly names (Drummydoodles), pedestrian names (Tabby), and names that prefigured twentieth-century media (Buffy and Tootsie). Cats hunt rodents, so the population of voles, chipmunks, and other burrowing beasts decrease in inverse proportion to the felines on the property.

🐾 Oscar, the modern-day museum cat, greeted many visitors in the spirit of Vinnie's pets.

🐾 RIGHT Lavinia Dickinson in later life with one of her cats, standing outside the kitchen door.

Down the flagstone path, the fruit trees begin to set. Cherries, apples, plums, and pears, still in miniature, swell in the aftermath of spring blooms. The fruit on the three cherry trees closest to the house will be the first to ripen. Delicious just picked, they yield pies for the table, once pitted. The fruit attracts the birds, taking bids on the sugary drupes.

In addition to fruit trees, the Dickinson garden also has a strawberry bed. The classic varieties bear heavily for a few weeks in June, sometimes a quart per plant. It is time for preserves and baking, the smell of cooking strawberries wafting out of the kitchen door and into the garden.

Over the fence -
Strawberries - grow -
Over the fence -
I could climb - if I tried, I know -
Berries are nice!

But - if I stained my Apron -
God would certainly scold!
Oh, dear, - I guess if He were a Boy -
He'd - climb - if He could!

271, 1861

In the lower garden, the borders are lush. The various siblings of the carnation family are all in bloom. To Mary Bowles, the droll Dickinson once queried, "How is your garden – Mary? Are the Pinks true – and the Sweet Williams faithful?" The edges of pinks (*Dianthus caryophyllus*) are zig-zag, like a seam that has been trimmed with pinking shears. Their gray strappy leaves grow in a mat. Their small pink flowers are edible, lovely sprinkled on top of cheese or a frosted teacake. Sometimes Dickinson called them gilliflowers, from the French word for cloves, since they smell spicy. Her forebears would have used them to flavor wine and ale.

"Are the Pinks true?" Painting by Orra White Hitchcock.

The sweet williams (*Dianthus barbatus*), another cottage garden flower, open in shades of white, pink, and magenta. In Dickinson's garden, the sweet williams are sometimes unfaithful, disappearing after a year or two. But if she planted new seeds each summer, they'd behave biennially, growing green one year and blooming the next. Jewels for the garden.

When Diamonds are a Legend,
And Diadems - a Tale -
I Brooch and Earrings for Myself,
Do sow, and Raise for sale -

And tho' I'm scarce accounted,
My Art, a Summer Day - had Patrons -
Once - it was a Queen -
And once - a Butterfly -

553, 1863

Perennials hold the dominion in Dickinson's early summer borders. They seem to open all at once, vying for attention. The poppies wave with vigor, bible-paper-thin petals on wiry stems. If they are happy in the garden, they sow seeds from their ornamental seed heads and pop up in unexpected places. The red poppies look like miniature suns.

It was a quiet seeming Day -
There was no harm in earth or sky -
Till with the setting sun
There strayed an accidental Red
A Strolling Hue, one would have said
To westward of the Town -

But when the Earth begun to jar
And Houses vanished with a roar
And Human Nature hid
We comprehended by the Awe
As those that Dissolution saw
The Poppy in the Cloud -

1442, 1877

White daisies with yellow eyes contrast with red poppies. Dickinson associated with them, sometimes taking Daisy as a nickname for herself in letters. The daisies that she grew and that still populate the fields around Amherst are oxeye daisies. While she adored them, not everyone agreed. One of her relations countered, "Why do people rave over the beauty of daisies? They look to me like hard-boiled eggs cut in two." Flowers are a matter of taste.

As summer progresses, the lilies open with fanfare. The blooms are preceded by dense tufts of green each spring that extend into green leafy stalks. Trumpet-shaped flowers return reliably year after year. Dickinson grew an array of lilies, a spectacle in the garden for weeks. There were many varieties including an alluring, unnamed "white one with rose-powdered petals and brown velvet stamens, far more elaborate than the simple varieties," plus Japanese lilies, yellow lilies, Madonna lilies, and tiger lilies.

Emily Dickinson knew her Bible from years of reading her King James, a present from her father. She quoted gardening passages from both testaments when it suited her. References to "Consider the lilies" (Luke 12:27; Matthew 6:28), appear a half-dozen times in her letters, often with gifts of flowers. With a flair for exaggeration, she once confessed "the only Commandment I ever obeyed – 'Consider the Lilies.'"

She must have felt that she knew the lily in a biblical sense. "Must it not have enthralled the Bible, if we may infer from its selection?" Dickinson wrote to her friend, Maria Whitney, "'The lily of the field!' I never pass one without being chagrined for Solomon, and so in love with 'the lily' anew, that were I sure no one saw me, I might make those advances which in after life I should repent." She did have a way with lilies. One year while staying with her favorite cousins, Louisa ("Loo") and Frances ("Fanny") Norcross, in Boston, she noted the progress of a particular flower and reported to Vinnie, "The Pink Lily you gave Loo, has had five flowers since I came, and has more Buds. The Girls think it my influence."

Like lilies, foxgloves are vertical accents in Dickinson's summer garden. From fuzzy leaves around the base of the plant, their magenta

🌾 A yellow lily worthy of the commandment Dickinson invoked, in a painting by Clarissa Munger Badger.

buds open along stems upright as obelisks. As the flowers suited fairy tales, they are called fox, or folk's, gloves. Whether fox, fairy, or mere mortal, the blooms look inviting to fingers. Even its botanical name, *Digitalis*, refers to fingers, our ten digits. Look inside the blooms and you'll see lovely spotting, a neon sign outside a pub for pollinators.

It was rare for Dickinson to have a poem published, but one appeared in 1861 in the *Springfield Republican* with the title "The May Wine." Featuring foxglove and bees, it can be read as her poetic response to one of Emerson's essays. She had read this passage in his *Second Series*, "The Poet," written by the Congregationalist minister-turned-author from Concord:

🌼 Tiger lilies, botanically *Lilium superbum*, nod their heads in the summer garden.

> *The poet knows that he speaks adequately, then, only when he speaks somewhat wildly, or, "with the flower of the mind"; not with the intellect used as organ, but with the intellect released from all service, and suffered to take its direction from its celestial life; or as the ancients were wont to express themselves, not with the intellect alone, but with the intellect inebriated by nectar.*

Dickinson's antiphon was ecstatic.

I taste a liquor never brewed -
From Tankards scooped in Pearl -
Not all the Frankfort Berries
Yield such an Alcohol!

Inebriate of air - am I -
And Debauchee of Dew -
Reeling - thro' endless summer days -
From inns of molten Blue -

When "Landlords" turn the drunken Bee
Out of the Foxglove's door -
When Butterflies - renounce their "drams" -
I shall but drink the more!

Till Seraphs swing their snowy Hats -
And Saints - to windows run -
To see the little Tippler
Leaning against the - Sun!

207, 1861

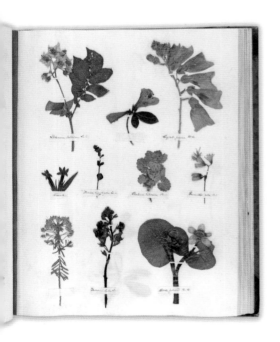

Annuals are workhorses of summer borders including the garden at the Homestead. While perennials return every year for a repeat performance, with rare exception they bloom for a few weeks only. An annual on the other hand is determined to set seed this season, so boosts its blooms. A combination of annuals and perennials like Emily and Vinnie planted in their garden ensures that something is always in flower, attracting people and pollinators.

⚘ The foxglove shows its bee-enticing flowers, pressed into the herbarium on the top right of page twenty-nine.

Summer Annuals

SNAPDRAGON (*Antirrhinum majus*). Rising with spires of pink, white, and magenta, even yellow, the snapdragons add to the foxgloves in late June. They seem more affectionate than their persnickety name suggests. If you squeeze the back of a bloom, it will open and close—an expressive mouth speaking to the inner child of every gardener.

GLOBE AMARANTH (*Gomphrena globosa*). Dickinson often explored the subject of immortality in her poems as well as her plants. Among the herbarium pages, you will find several flowers used especially for dried flower arranging. Native to Central America, globe amaranth produces round purple flowers all summer until frost. Dry them for

winter, and they retain their form and color. Other annual "everlastings" in the herbarium are strawflower (*Xerochrysum bracteatum*) and winged everlasting (*Ammobium alatum*).

SWEET ALYSSUM (*Lobularia maritima*). If summer is the sea, then alyssum is the foam on the waves. It is a tiny plant, only about three inches tall, with a haze of minute flowers, most often white, but also pink and purple. They smell sweet and add a lacy trimming along the front edge of a flower garden. If you have

⚘ Annual globe amaranth and perennial feverfew weave together in the Homestead's summer garden.

a flagstone path, sow sweet alyssum seeds along the stones. They like to send their roots down into the cool damp spaces. Alyssum will often self-sow if it is happy. Dickinson gathered seeds of sweet alyssum and mignonette from her fall garden to grow indoors over the winter to scent the conservatory air.

MIGNONETTE (*Reseda odorata*). Pronounced with the accent firmly on the "–ette," the word mignonette emphasizes as only the French can the diminutive size of its flowers. The inflorescence is evasive, small and, to the eye, inconspicuous. It is downright demure. But it broadcasts its fragrance like a department store perfume counter. As Emily Dickinson walked through the garden, the aroma of mignonette would waft toward her, directing eye to follow nose. Brought inside to scent a bouquet, it was the nineteenth-century equivalent of an air freshener. It's still grown commercially in France for the perfume industry. You won't find mignonette in anything but a specialty nursery, so if you want it in your garden, you'll need to grow it each year from seed.

STOCK (*Matthiola incana*). Another fragrant flower in the Dickinson garden, stock is a member of the mustard family. It is grown for pastel blooms that look like clusters of miniature roses. There are tall varieties for cutting, medium varieties for the border, and dwarf varieties for edging. Like Goldilocks, Dickinson could choose the one that was just right for her garden. And she enjoyed word play with "stocks," both financial and floral.

✹ In Dickinson's portfolio "spicy 'stocks'" vied with "Daffodil Dowries."

SWEET SULTAN (*Amberboa moschata*). If we only knew the potentate for which this flower was named. They are fragrant, hardy annuals that grow in the warm weather, blooming with composite flowers that look a bit like thistles. They grow as tall as a yardstick so keep them toward the back of the border and use them for cutting and drying. They keep flowering until frost if deadheaded regularly. In Dickinson's time, sweet sultans were most often purple, pink, and blue, but now you can also buy seeds in a range of white and yellow.

🌿 Red clover, christened "the Purple Democrat" in Dickinson's poem.

The Dickinson flower garden does not have a monopoly on the butterflies. The meadow across Main Street is full of red clover (*Trifolium pratense*). Brought to America by European colonists for their cattle, it is a preferred flower of many pollinators. It is also good for the soil, as all varieties of clover (and other members of the bean family) capture nitrogen from the air onto their roots. A natural alchemy.

There is a flower that Bees prefer -
And Butterflies - desire -
To gain the Purple Democrat
The Humming Bird - aspire -

And Whatsoever Insect pass -
A Honey bear away
Proportioned to his several dearth
And her - capacity -

Her face be rounder than the Moon
And ruddier than the Gown
Of Orchis in the Pasture -
Or Rhododendron - worn -

She doth not wait for June -
Before the World be Green -
Her sturdy little Countenance
Against the Wind - be seen -

Contending with the Grass -
Near Kinsman to Herself -
For privilege of Sod and Sun -
Sweet Litigants for Life -

And when the Hills be full -
And newer fashions blow -
Doth not retract a single spice
For pang of jealousy -

Her Public - be the Noon -
Her Providence - the Sun -
Her Progress - by the Bee - proclaimed -
In sovereign - Swerveless Tune -

The Bravest - of the Host -
Surrendering - the last -
Nor even of Defeat - aware -
When cancelled by the Frost -

642, 1863

Dickinson ventured beyond her garden beds in summer, meandering in field and forest. She collected on her walks, both poetically and
literally. The ferns in the landscape around Amherst grew in clumps
and swathes, their fiddleheads completely unfurled in summer. People
dug them up for house and garden, and gathered and pressed them for

✿ Daisies, buttercups, and red clover, from Clarissa Munger
Badger's *Wildflowers Drawn and Colored from Nature*.

FERN & WOOD MOSS

❧ "A Fern from my own Forest."

❧ A fern "on untravelled roads," painted by Orra White Hitchcock.

a bit of nature indoors. In one missive Dickinson wrote, "I bring you a Fern from my own Forest – where I play every Day." The fern enclosed in the letter was a rock polypody (*Polypodium virginianum*), a small native species that grows on moist rocks and in rock walls. If you turn the fern over, you can see its round sori, its spore-bearing polka dots all over the underside.

Ferns are part of the unfolding of the season, including the hay-scented fern that carpets the local Amherst woods. Brush them with your hand to smell the fresh aroma.

An altered look about the hills -
A Tyrian light the village fills -
A wider sunrise in the morn -
A deeper twilight on the lawn -
A print of a vermillion foot -
A purple finger on the slope -
A flippant fly opon the pane -
A spider at his trade again -
An added strut in Chanticleer -

A flower expected everywhere -
An axe shrill singing in the woods -
Fern odors on untravelled roads -
All this and more I cannot tell -
A furtive look you know as well -
And Nicodemus' Mystery
Receives it's annual reply!

90, 1859

Summer is the start of mushroom season. They seem to pop up overnight, a characteristic that Dickinson noted. In her day, the mushroom was classified with plants, rather than fungi. Today's botany informs us that the mushroom is old, with vast underground networks, like an extended family. Gazing at a mushroom is a prurient affair, given that it is the reproductive organ of a much larger plant. For Dickinson it was entertaining. Magic.

The Mushroom is the Elf of Plants -
At Evening it is not
At Morning, in a truffled Hut
It stop opon a Spot

As if it tarried always
And yet it's whole Career
Is shorter than a Snake's Delay
And fleeter than a Tare -

'Tis Vegetation's Juggler -
The Joy of Alibi -
Doth like a Bubble antedate
And like a Bubble hie -

I feel as if the Grass was pleased
To have it intermit -
This surreptitious Scion
Of Summer's circumspect.

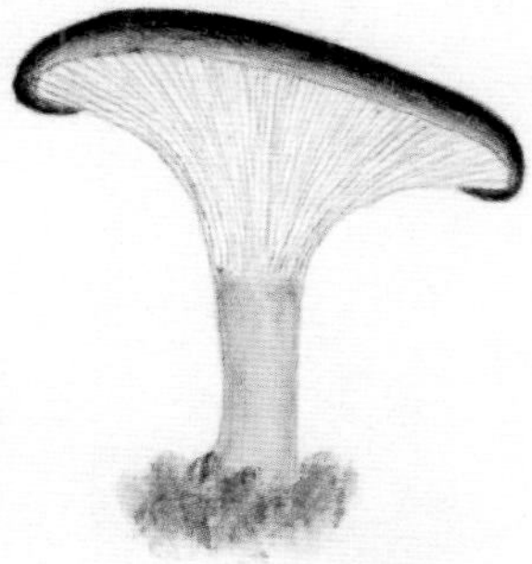

An "Elf of Plants," painted by Orra White Hitchcock.

Had Nature any supple Face -
Or could she one contemn -
Had Nature an Apostate -
That Mushroom - it is Him!

1350, 1874

In the wetlands the waterlily is in bloom. Waterlilies are ancient plants, primitives, never leaving the marshes where they evolved. Once, when her classmates dubbed Vinnie "the Pond Lily," Emily Dickinson retorted, "Then I am the Cow Lily." Like the two Dickinson sisters, both waterlilies are from the same family but are very different. The pond lily is showy with large white flowers, up to six inches across. The cow lily (*Nuphar advena*) is subdued, with small, waxy yellow flowers in the shallows of ponds and lakes and in sluggish streams. Both have long roots that anchor the plants in the mud.

Will there really be a "morning"?
Is there such a thing as "Day"?
Could I see it from the mountains
If I were tall as they?

Has it feet like Water lilies?
Has it feathers like a Bird?
Is it brought from famous countries
Of which I have never heard?

Oh some Scholar! Oh some Sailor!
Oh some Wise Man from the skies!
Please to tell a little Pilgrim
Where the place called "morning" lies!

148, 1860

With late summer yawning ahead in Amherst, the frost is still far off.

Late Summer

A HEDGE AWAY

BY HER LATE THIRTIES, Emily Dickinson withdrew. It was gradual and self-imposed. Unique rather than tragic, Dickinson styled herself "a Balboa of house and garden." A garden is a safe harbor for a land-locked Balboa. Plants are accepting of eccentricities.

I hav'nt told my garden yet -
Lest that should conquer me.
I hav'nt quite the strength now
To break it to the Bee -

I will not name it in the street
For shops w'd stare at me -
That one so shy - so ignorant
Should have the face to die.

The hillsides must not know it -
Where I have rambled so -
Nor tell the loving forests
The day that I shall go -

Nor lisp it at the table -
Nor heedless by the way
Hint that within the Riddle
One will walk today -

40, 1858

🌿 The ground which Dickinson no longer crossed "for any House or town."

In 1869, Emily Dickinson wrote to a gentleman she was hoping to meet in person that she would have to decline his invitation to a literary soirée in Boston. "Could it please your convenience to come so far as Amherst I should be very glad," she offered, adding, "but I do not cross my Father's ground for any House or town."

Her correspondent was Thomas Wentworth Higginson, who in later years would become a key player in the Dickinson publication chronicles. A renaissance man, Higginson was a Unitarian minister, abolitionist, and women's rights activist, as well as a regular writer for *The Atlantic Monthly*, a new magazine subscribed to by the Dickinson household. He wrote about an array of topics—nature, flowers, and, in April 1862, an essay entitled "Letter to a Young Contributor," giving advice to prospective authors. The piece had provoked an unusual response in Dickinson. She sent a letter enclosing four of her poems and asking, "Are you too deeply occupied to say if my Verse is alive?" It was the first of seventy-one letters she wrote to Higginson. As she had hoped, he became her mentor, her "Preceptor" as she later called him.

Higginson did find time to "come so far as Amherst" in 1870, one year after her invitation and almost a decade after their first exchange. On a warm Tuesday afternoon in August, he waited in the front parlor of the Dickinson Homestead. He described it to his wife in a letter. "A large country lawyer's house, brown brick, with great trees & a garden—I sent up my card," he wrote, "A parlor dark & cool & stiffish, a few books & engravings & an open piano." As he waited, he perused the bookshelves and, like any author, was glad to find copies of some of the books he had written. Then Emily Dickinson came through the door.

Continuing the letter to his wife that night, he portrayed the poet as a small woman with reddish hair and plain face in a simple dress of "exquisitely clean white pique & a blue net worsted shawl." Dickinson's opening gambit was striking. "She came to me with two day lilies which she put in a sort of childlike way into my hand & said, 'These are my introduction.'" They had a long conversation, and he returned to the house that evening for another. He closed the letter, summing up Dickinson's intensity, "I never was with any one who drained my nerve power so much."

❧ Dickinson's mentor, Thomas Wentworth Higginson, though older than he was when they met.

❧ The daylily, a bold flower for a first meeting, painted by Helen Sharp.

Dickinson's daylily introduction might have been due to a preference for their open, orange blooms, or she might have been communicating with a floral vocabulary. She once wrote, "Let me thank the little Cousin in flowers, which without lips, have language." The language of flowers was the rage. It was important to have the same lexicon if you were exchanging messages via flowers. In one dictionary daylily meant flirt, in another, beauty. It seems unlikely that with her daylilies she was being provocative with the married Mr. Higginson. But one can't know.

<x Old-fashioned "species" daylilies blooming in the garden at the Homestead.

At times Emily Dickinson seemed to prefer the voices of flowers over those of people. Writing to Susan, she once reported, "I am from the fields, you know, and while quite at home with the Dandelion, make but sorry figure in a Drawing-room." Wandering the area with her dog, Carlo, she avoided chance encounters, preferring plants to people. As she described to Higginson:

> Of "Men and Women" – they talk of Hallowed things, aloud, and embarrass my Dog – He and I dont object to them, if they'll exist their side. I think Carl[o] would please you – He is dumb, and brave – I think you would like the Chestnut Tree, I met in my walk. It hit my notice suddenly – and I thought the Skies were in Blossom.

While she shunned society, Dickinson was at home in her garden, outdoors or in. When her father remodeled the brick mansion, he had added a conservatory. It became Dickinson's domain. Carpenters and masons had attached the conservatory to the southeast corner of the brick house. Built over the exterior walls and encompassing the dining room windows, Dickinson called it her "garden off the dining room." At just six feet wide and seventeen feet long, the small glass room could make do with passive heat from the house.

With the dining room windows open, heat from the Franklin stove could fill the conservatory and keep the plants from freezing. White shelves spanned the dining room windows. Three double-paned windows stretched from floor to ceiling, enclosing it to the south. Two glass doors opened to the outside: one led down stone steps into the garden, the other led to the street through a gate in the fence.

The interior entrance to the conservatory was through her father's study.

BELOW Dickinson's "garden off the dining room," in a photograph from 1915.

Like many good Victorians, Emily Dickinson was a magpie when it came to her plant collection, but she had standards. "She tolerated none of the usual variety of mongrel house plants," her niece later remembered. "A rare scarlet lily, a resurrection calla, perhaps—and here it was always summer with the oxalis dripping from hanging baskets like humble incense upon the heads of the household and its frequenters."

Dickinson inventoried the conservatory in a letter to her cousins:

*Crocuses come up, in the garden off
the dining room . . . and a fuchsia,
that pussy partook, mistaking it for
strawberries. And that we have primroses – like the little pattern sent in last
winter's note – and heliotropes by the
aprons full, the mountain colored one
– and a Jessamine bud, you know the
little odor like Lubin, – and gilliflowers,
magenta, and few mignonette and sweet
alyssum bountiful, and carnation buds.*

(Lubin was a famous Parisian
perfumer.)

A conservatory creates a pleasant
but steady round of work. Plants require
tending: trimming, turning, potting up.
Gardeners create strange intersecting
worlds of desert and jungle. Cacti demand
drought. Ferns demand moisture. Dickinson

✿ Oxalis, painted by Orra White Hitchcock.

✿ BELOW It takes attentiveness and
diligence for conservatory plants to thrive.

sometimes got the watering done with a Tom Sawyer technique. "She let me water her plants in her little conservatory—Cape jasmine, heliotrope, and ferns," her niece wrote, "reaching up to the higher shelves by a tiny watering-pot with a long, slender spout like the antennae of insects, which had been made for her after an idea of her father's."

The bright light in Dickinson's indoor garden signaled plants to set buds. Sharing some of her conservatory's bounty, she once wrote, "I send you inland buttercups as out-door flowers are still at sea." Her inland plants were varied, exotic, erotic.

I tend my flowers for thee -
Bright Absentee!
My Fuschzia's Coral Seams
Rip - while the Sower - dreams -

Geraniums - tint - and spot -
Low Daisies - dot -
My Cactus - splits her Beard
To show her throat -

Carnations - tip their spice -
And Bees - pick up -
A Hyacinth - I hid -
Puts out a Ruffled Head -
And odors fall
From flasks - so small -
You marvel how they held -

Globe Roses - break their satin flake -
Opon my Garden floor -
Yet - thou - not there -
I had as lief they bore -
No crimson - more -

From 367, 1862

The conservatory's confined space concentrated floral scents. "My flowers are near and foreign," she announced to her friend Elizabeth Holland in a letter one early March day, "and I have but to cross the floor to stand in the Spice Isles. The wind blows gay today and the Jays bark like Blue Terriers."

While the conservatory was Emily's province, she did share it. "Vinnie is happy with her duties, her pussies, and her posies, for the little garden within, though tiny, is triumphant. There are scarlet carnations, with a witching suggestion, and hyacinths covered with promises which I know they will keep." The Dickinson sisters shared the outdoor garden as well, and one wonders if they always agreed. For Vinnie "all her flowers did as they liked: tyrannized over her, hopped out of their own beds into each other's beds, were never reproved or removed as long as they bloom; for a live flower to . . . Lavinia was more than any dead horticultural principle." Lavinia Dickinson seems to have been a gardener with a laissez-faire approach.

As her sister became more reclusive, Vinnie also stepped in as her public face to Amherst. Vinnie transacted the commerce with people outside of the intimate Dickinson circle. She directed the workmen in the garden and requisitioned supplies. It was Miss Lavinia who gave the orders and paid the bills, giving her older sister much-needed privacy.

Vinnie dealt with garden requests as well, contributing flowers for funerals and weddings and to local girls who needed a bouquet for a ball. Arriving at the Homestead, you would often find her in the garden. A gentleman once did. She later recounted the incident to her niece, "I had on my most bog-mire clothes – my worst hat, the ends of my shawl tied around my waist Gypsy fashion, – only my white gauntlets were reputable; but I offered him a seat in James' wheel barrow, hoping he would prefer it to the parlor." We get a window onto Lavinia's gardening garb and to the gardener who was helping her with the heavy work.

A SELECTION *OF*
EMILY DICKINSON'S
Conservatory Plants

CAPE JASMINE (*Gardenia jasminoides* 'Veitchii'). Dickinson would send friends a bloom of cape jasmine—what we generally call gardenia—to mark a special occasion. Her niece called it "her crowning attention." Gardenias can be fickle plants, but Dickinson was clearly up to the challenge. At their best, their shiny leaves and sultry white blooms are fit for royalty.

DAPHNE (*Daphne odora*). As you might expect from its odoriferous epithet, daphne is prized for its fragrance. To the ancients, Daphne was a naiad—a nymph of flowing water—pursued by Apollo and transformed into a shrub to avoid his unwanted advances. On the occasion of Thomas Wentworth Higginson's second visit to the Dickinson Homestead in 1873, the poet floated in with a sprig.

FUCHSIA (*Fuchsia hybrida*). The plant that Dickinson grew was named for Leonhart Fuchs, a sixteenth-century German professor of medicine, who first described it botanically. Species hail from the South Pacific, Central and South America, and the Caribbean. Pink, red, and purple bells hang down, making fuchsia a great choice to drape over the edge of conservatory shelves. It benefits from pruning even if one of Vinnie's cats isn't around to eat it. Pinching back the soft new growth encourages the plant to push outside shoots and bloom profusely.

✻ Ornamental wood sorrel (*Oxalis triangularis*), growing in the Dickinson's conservatory.

✻ Fuchsia "that pussy partook."

OLEANDER (*Nerium oleander*). If Dickinson had written murder mysteries, this plant could have been featured prominently, since all parts are poisonous. But if you ignore its toxic aspects, oleander is a lovely greenhouse plant or tender annual for northern climes. Its leaves are glossy and evergreen with feathery pink blooms clustered at the ends of its stems. The Dickinsons moved the potted oleander out to the piazza in summer.

WOOD SORREL (*Oxalis*). Many species of wood sorrel are grown as ornamental plants and a half dozen are native to Massachusetts. Their five-petaled blooms are prolific—white, magenta, apricot, yellow—depending on the type. Wood sorrels are also edible, if somewhat sour. Like rhubarb and spinach, they are high in oxalic acid.

🌿 The young and dashing Austin Dickinson (left), and
Susan Gilbert Dickinson, "Sister Sue" (right).

There were three gardening sisters. After Austin's marriage in
1856, Emily wrote a poem opening, "One Sister have I in our house –
and one a hedge away." The sister a metaphorical hedge-width distant
was her sister-in-law, Susan Gilbert Dickinson. She was a long-time
friend of all three Dickinson siblings. In 1852, Emily wrote Susan,
commenting, "I have to go out in the garden now, and whip a Crown-
Imperial for presuming to hold it's head up, until you have come
home." This is a regal comparison, as crown imperials dominate the
border with stems as tall as yardsticks topped
with bright red or yellow flowers.

Looking out of her bedroom window to the
west, Dickinson could see Austin and Susan's
elaborate house next door—The Evergreens.
Before they married, the couple considered flying
the familial coop to resettle in the Midwest near
Susan's brothers in Michigan. Their "go west"
yearning was a widespread western fever. In
the decades after the Erie Canal opened the rich
Ohio River Valley, farmers in rural New England

🌿 The striking bloom of
the crown imperial.

abandoned their acres of hill and stone for the flatter greener pastures and deep prairie soils. With the agricultural exodus went tradesmen and professionals.

Instead of westward ho, Edward Dickinson enticed Austin and Susan to stay. He dangled two carrots: he would make Austin a partner in his law practice, and he would build the couple a house in a style of their choice on his substantial adjoining lot. The path between the houses symbolizes a life choice and a financial bargain.

The couple set out to make a showplace. The architecture of their "cottage" was the trendy Italianate. From its square tower, they could survey

🌿 The Evergreens in a later picture, circa 1920.

the Amherst landscape and get a bird's-eye view of their own garden. They decorated the house in the latest chic with a dowry from Susan's brothers. The name that they gave the house, The Evergreens, reflected their gardening interests.

A new and elegant picket fence defined the combined Dickinson properties. In front of the Homestead and The Evergreens, the fence had gates for people and gates for horses, carriages, and wagons. To leave a gate open was a misdemeanor in Edward Dickinson's book, and Austin shared his father's view. Should a neighborhood boy forget to shut it, he "was almost certain to hear a stentorian voice in the distance saying in accents none too mild, 'Boy, shut that gate.'" Austin Dickinson had spotted him from the garden or piazza.

In addition to installing the fence, the Dickinsons planted the first hemlock hedge in the spring of 1865. Emily, staying at the time with cousins in Boston, wrote home to Vinnie, "I hope the Chimneys are done and the Hemlocks set, and the Two Teeth filled, in the Front yard – How astonishing it will be to me." The "Two Teeth" were the pointed ornamental posts holding the entrance gate at the front walk.

 Austin and Susan Dickinson's home, The Evergreens, was the first named house in Amherst.

 RIGHT The fence and hedge in front of the Dickinson property.

Edward and Austin directed the men to be sure that the hedge would be set straight. Hemlock (*Tsuga canadensis*) was an excellent choice. Native to the Amherst area, it tolerates shade from maturing broadleaf trees and can be shaped by shearing. The Dickinson hedge was a green arm enclosing the property and a dark backdrop for more colorful plants.

> A Lady red, amid the Hill
> Her annual secret keeps!
> A Lady white, within the Field
> In placid Lily sleeps!

The tidy Breezes, with their Brooms
Sweep vale, and hill, and tree!
Prithee, my pretty Housewives!
Who may expected be?

The neighbors do not yet suspect!
The woods exchange a smile!
Orchard, and Buttercup, and Bird -
In such a little while!

And yet, how still the Landscape stands!
How nonchalant the Hedge!
As if the "Resurrection"
Were nothing very strange!

137, 1860

The path between the houses was well trod, and sister Emily was a frequent visitor at The Evergreens. "It was here that she would fly to the piano, if the mood required, and thunder out a composition of her own which she laughingly but appropriately called 'The Devil,'" one of her contemporaries remembered. She visited day and night. "When her father came, lantern in hand, to see that she reached home in safety, she would elude him and dart through the darkness to reach home before him." Nocturnal Amherst would have been dark, lit only by the phased moon.

A daytime stroll around The Evergreens was a walk through a landscape styled in a mid- to late- century cut. Gardens are subject to fashion, and The Evergreens was romantic and picturesque. Stone steps and two terraces led up from Main Street to the front door, framed with masses of rhododendron and English hawthorn. Beds were curved, shrubbery massed. Views were composed with trees and shrubs, visually pleasing from the doors, windows, and gates.

Borders blurred between indoors and out. On the west side of the house, Austin and Susan designed their piazza around an ancient apple tree, leaving an opening in the roof for its gnarled branches. A vine clambered up to drape the porch roofline with bloom and

A path later described by Austin and Susan's eldest child as "just wide enough for two who love."

greenery. On the lawn, another apple tree was transformed into a living summerhouse. To reach its built-in seat—six feet above ground—one climbed a set of wooden stairs. There were benches set in the lawn, adding interest and places to rest and contemplate. Emily must have been delighted to watch the transformation.

Austin spent much of his spare time in the garden and was something of a horticultural sophisticate. He followed trends in landscape gardening, including the writings of Andrew Jackson Downing who advocated the picturesque style. To flank The Evergreens, Austin planted banks of rhododendrons. He collected ferns on his outings. One that long grew in the shade of The Evergreens was the royal fern (*Osmunda regalis*). A stately monarch of the fern world, it couldn't have gotten there on its own, as its native habitat is more swampy terrain in Amherst and surrounds. Royal fern, like much of the plant world, is adaptable and adjusted to its new home on the property.

Austin and Sue were well-connected and enjoyed entertaining in their new home. They welcomed guests at bloom time, for the rhododendron and magnolias in particular. Harriet Beecher Stowe dined there, as did Ralph Waldo Emerson. Frances Hodgson Burnett, a well-known author of the day who later wrote *The Secret Garden*, dined there in 1880. Burnett wrote in her journal that in the middle of the luncheon Emily Dickinson sent her "a strange wonderful little poem" nestled on a bed of heart's ease and presented in a bowl.

Other guests included Frederick Law Olmsted and Calvert Vaux, the already-famous designers of New York's Central Park. The Dickinsons hosted them on many occasions at The Evergreens, partaking of Susan's elegant menus. Susan recalled the men talking of landscape possibilities and plants—growth habit, form, and particulars so detailed that the species seemed to animate. At the supper table one evening, discussing a particular blue spruce, "the men with one accord left the table to examine it at the extreme end of the grounds, returning twenty minutes later, still completely absorbed in their subject, and quite regardless of the hiatus in the meal." Vaux later sent his book, *Villas and Cottages*, inscribed to Susan.

Ignatz Pilat, the Austrian-trained botanical superintendent of Central Park, also visited, staying for several days. Pilat accompanied them on an excursion up Mount Warner in nearby Hadley. During their outing he dug up a bracken fern and showed Susan the distinctive double-headed eagle in the cross section of its roots and shoots.

While his sister Emily collected plants for her flower garden, herbarium, and conservatory, Austin Dickinson was working on a larger scale. He planted trees, unusual trees. Like many gentlemen of the day, he viewed his property as something of an arboretum. He created, by all accounts, a beautiful result.

Susan added flower borders and, on the sunny west slope near the house, glass growing frames. In one of her beds, a rose called 'Baltimore Belle' stretched out its canes with clusters of light pink flowers in June and bright orange hips in the fall. She underplanted the roses with purple heliotrope and the soft grayish leaves of scented geranium.

A talented flower arranger, Susan gathered flowers for the table and for tiny buttonhole bouquets to adorn the gentlemen's lapels. She also harvested for her menus. In describing one May luncheon, she wrote, "Fresh asparagus and salad from our own garden and hotbed made an appetizing garnish for the luncheon. Arbutus filled the center of the table, bright sunshine looked in at all the windows, as if eager to rival the sparkle of the talk within." Whether she cut the asparagus from her own garden or from the Homestead's next door is not known.

Against a stand of conifers between the houses, Susan planted a skyline of hollyhocks. By late summer the flower stalks were taller than Austin, with wide single blooms opening from the bottom up. Children like to make dolls out of the flowers—turned upside down, the petals look like colorful skirts. Hollyhocks drop

❧ Perhaps Susan Dickinson's boutonnieres looked like this one, painted by Orra White Hitchcock.

their skirts when they are finished blooming. "I am very busy picking up stems and stamens as the hollyhocks leave their clothes around," Dickinson once noted. Perhaps she helped to pick up actual clothes at The Evergreens, too, as the family was growing.

Dickinson wrote to a friend of an impromptu procession on the property, "Sue – draws her little Boy – pleasant days – in a Cab – and Carlo walks behind, accompanied by a Cat – from each Establishment – It looks funny to see so small a man, going out of Austin's House." Two more children followed, and their voices began to animate the gardens. Austin and Sue had three: Edward in 1861, Martha in 1866, and, much later, Gilbert, born in 1875. Ned, Mattie, and Gib. A normal, rambunctious crew, they were a joy to their aunt.

Ned pilfered from neighboring orchards on occasion. Dickinson sent a note from next door. "We have all heard of the Boy whose Constitution required stolen fruit, though his Father's Orchard was loaded," she admonished, but then added, "There was something in the unlawfulness that gave it a saving flavor." Mattie, the middle child, sometimes skipped church and spent time with Aunt Emily in the conservatory or the garden. The youngest, Gib, once stopped by with a request, but found his aunt asleep. When she woke, she came to The Evergreens with this response, "Aunt Emily waked up now, and brought this little Plant all the way from her Crib for Gilbert to carry to his Teacher – Good Night – Aunt Emily's asleep again." There is nothing like children to enliven a garden.

Written messages passed back and forth between the houses. Timothy, the hired hand, walked foaming pails of milk from the Homestead's cows to The Evergreens. The children watched his approach in anticipation until their mother released them. Had Aunt Emily sent anything along? Mattie remembered fondly:

> Oftenest it was a cardboard box, and Tim said, as we took it from him, "From Miss Im'ly." In it would be perhaps three tiny frosted, heart-shaped cakes, or some of her chocolate caramels—with a flower on top, heliotrope, a red lily, or cape jasmine—and underneath always a note or a poem for our mother."

The neighborhood children joined Ned, Mattie, and Gib, playing on the property around both houses. In later life, they remembered the gardens, orchard, and outbuildings as perfect settings for gypsy camps or pirate adventures. They all knew Miss Emily. One of the group, MacGregor Jenkins, grew up to remember, "She was not shy with [us] . . . she was a splendid comrade and a stanch companion. Her ready smile, her dancing eyes, her quick reply made us all tingle with pleasure when we were near her."

Miss Emily knew how to entertain the neighborhood gang. In a designated post office in the hedge, she traded secret messages with the sometimes pirates, sometimes gypsies. She would lower gingerbread in a basket from her bedroom window. They would put in a daisy or clover in return. "We knew the things she loved best," Jenkins recalled, "and we sought the early wild flowers, a flaming leaf, a glistening stone, the shining, fallen feather of a bird and took them to her, sure of her appreciation of the gift as well as the giving." Though Dickinson had given up her wildflower wanderings, she still had emissaries to bring her treasures.

She must have been an interesting puzzle to a child. "She had a habit of standing in rapt attention as if she were listening to something very faint and far off," wrote Jenkins. "We children often saw her at sunset, standing at the kitchen window, peering through a vista in the trees to the western sky—her proud little head thrown back, her eyes raised and one hand held characteristically before her." To some of the little girls, Dickinson wrote a gardening fable:

> Which shall it be, Geraniums or Juleps?
> The butterfly up in the sky that hasn't any name
> And hasn't any tax to pay and hasn't any home
> Is just as high as you and I, and higher, I believe
> So soar away and never sigh
> For that's the way to grieve.

It was summer. Long days stretched to sunset, butterflies meandered, and geraniums bloomed in her garden.

Late Summer in Emily Dickinson's Garden

"Old Testament weather"

THE HEAT IN THE GARDEN HAS ITS OWN PRESENCE. In August, the mercury often lurks north of ninety. The air, dense with humidity, seems to slow everything down. These are the dog days, so named for the rising of Sirius the Dog Star, under whose influence the heat wags its tail, or hangs out its tongue. Dickinson seemed to relish it, though the garden and her sister disagreed. "The Days are very hot and the Weeds pant like the centre of Summer. They say the Corn likes it. I thought there were others besides the Corn. How deeply I was deluded! Vinnie rocks her Garden and moans that God wont help her." Thunderheads build up some afternoons, releasing their savage energy.

The Wind begun to rock the Grass
With threatening Tunes and low -
He threw a Menace at the Earth -
Another, at the Sky -
The Leaves unhooked themselves from Trees
And started all abroad -
The Dust did scoop itself like Hands
And throw away the Road -
The Wagons quickened on the streets
The Thunder hurried slow -
The Lightning showed a yellow Beak -
And then a livid Claw -
The Birds put up the Bars to Nests -
The Cattle clung to Barns -
Then came one Drop of Giant Rain
And then as if the Hands
That held the Dams, had parted hold,
The Waters wrecked the Sky,
But overlooked my Father's House -
Just Quartering a Tree -

796, 1864

Still, a dry spell is not uncommon. Dickinson noted its effect on the plants. "We are reveling in a gorgeous drought," she wrote. "The grass is painted brown, and how nature would look in other than the standard colors, we can all infer." As a gardener and a poet, she accepted weather extremes. Another day she indulged in metaphor, "Today is parched and handsome, though the Grass is the color of Statesmen's Shoes, and only the Butterfly rises to the situation." Dickinson also rose to the situation.

It's time to water in the garden. In the days before sprinkler systems and soaker hoses, Dickinson watered the old-fashioned way. One August, she reported, "Vinnie is trading with a Tin peddler – buying Water pots for me to sprinkle Geraniums with." She could fill them from a well out back near the barn.

What mystery pervades a well!
The water lives so far -
A neighbor from another world
Residing in a jar

Whose limit none have ever seen,
But just his lid of glass -
Like looking every time you please
In an abyss's face!

The grass does not appear afraid,
I often wonder he
Can stand so close and look so bold
At what is awe to me.

Related somehow they may be,
The sedge stands next the sea
Where he is floorless
And does no timidity betray -

But nature is a stranger yet;
The ones that cite her most

> Have never passed her haunted house,
> Nor simplified her ghost.
>
> To pity those that know her not
> Is helped by the regret
> That those who know her, know her less
> The nearer her they get.
>
> 1433, 1877

Mosquitoes whine, zeroing in on the gardener's exposed skin. Wrists and ankles make particular targets, even in those days when sleeves and skirts covered more of the gardener. A gardening hat was a required part of the costume, preventing an unfashionable suntan.

> Summer laid her simple Hat
> On it's boundless Shelf -
> Unobserved a Ribin dropt -
> Fasten it yourself.
>
> Summer laid her supple Glove
> In it's silvan Drawer -
> Wheresoe'er, or was she -
> The Affair of Awe -
>
> 1411, 1876

In the damp areas of the Dickinson meadow and on the banks of nearby streams, the cardinal flowers are blooming a luscious jewel red. In the wooded areas around both houses, the spring ephemeral wildflowers have withdrawn into their own subterranean homes. They escape into an early dormancy to avoid the summer heat. But later flowers emerge. Snowy eupatorium and white wood asters take their place.

Leaves on the trees are heavy, almost tired, the dark green of summer forgetting the spring chartreuse. Late in the day there is a subtle shift in the wind. The sky darkens with accumulating nimbus, and the change in air pressure makes the leaves blow upside down.

Summer laid
her simple Hat
On its boundless
Shelf.
Unobserved - a Ribbon
slipt
Fasten sanction
Summon it - yourself.

Summer laid her supple Glove
In its silvan Drawer -
Where soften the, or as
was she -
the
an
affairs
of Ane -
The Demand
of Ane

*Emily Dickinson
drafted many of her
poems on found paper—in
this case an unfolded envelope—
with possible variants and revisions.

The Leaves like Women, interchange
Sagacious Confidence -
Somewhat of Nods and somewhat
Portentous inference -

The Parties in both cases
Enjoining secrecy -
Inviolable compact
To notoriety.

1098, 1865

Across Main Street, the Dickinson meadow has its own "Sagacious
Confidence." An acquaintance from Emily's childhood wrote of the
meadow, "It was unbroken then by houses . . . The long grass was
filled with clover and buttercups and Queen Anne's lace, all swaying in
the breeze, a favorite haunt of bees and butterflies and bobolinks." It
is a haven for pollinators.

🌿 Cardinal flowers bloom red in late summer.
Painting by Clarissa Munger Badger.

🦋 This herbarium page includes the spiked blue lobelia, bottom center.

Butterflies feed in the meadow on the nectar of flowers that grow among the grasses. But by late summer, it's time to mow again. There is the whine of blade on whetstone. From her front windows, Dickinson could see the hired men swinging their scythes or the horses pulling a cutter, leaving swathes of mown grass like a wake from a boat. The wind brings the smell of cut grass.

The Wind did'nt come from the Orchard - today -
Further than that -
Nor stop to play with the Hay -
Nor threaten a Hat -
He's a transitive fellow - very -
Rely on that -
If He leave a Bur at the door
We know He has climbed a Fir -
But the Fir is Where - Declare -
Were you ever there?

If He brings Odors of Clovers -
And that is His business - not Our's -
Then He has been with the Mowers -
Whetting away the Hours
To sweet pauses of Hay -
His Way - of a June Day -

If He fling Sand, and Pebble -
Little Boy's Hats - and stubble -
With an occasional steeple -

And a hoarse "Get out of the Way, I say",
Who'd be the fool to stay?
Would you - Say -
Would you be the fool to stay?

494, 1862

When the clover hay came into the barn, Dickinson's niece and
nephews and the neighborhood children viewed it as an inalienable
right to climb the ladder to the loft and fling themselves onto the
sweet-smelling piles.

The Grass so little has to do -
A Sphere of simple Green -
With only Butterflies, to brood,
And Bees, to entertain -

And stir all day to pretty tunes
The Breezes fetch along,
And hold the Sunshine, in it's lap
And bow to everything,

And thread the Dews all night, like Pearl,
And make itself so fine
A Duchess, were too common
For such a noticing,

And even when it die, to pass
In odors so divine -
As lowly spices, gone to sleep -
Or Spikenards perishing -

And then to dwell in Sovereign Barns,
And dream the Days away,
The Grass so little has to do,
I wish I were a Hay -

379, 1862

Going out of the kitchen door, Dickinson could look up to her family's "Sovereign" barn. It was roomy enough to house a grinding wheel, the wood shed, a cabriolet lined in yellow broadcloth, and the sleigh. One or more hired men slept on the second floor above the tool storage. A wide center bay accommodated the hayloft and horse stalls. The wing to the west sheltered a milk cow, chickens, a pig. The animals in turn produced manure to enrich the garden. It was a pungent place in the heat.

Walking in her late summer garden, Dickinson noted, "The Weather is like Africa and the Flowers like Asia." Things were not only tropical, they'd gotten a bit out of hand. The beds were crawling with nasturtiums. Heliotropes and marigolds multiplied in the hot sun. Baby's breath expanded, a white haze above the rest of the garden. She sighed in a letter to Mary Bowles, "I've got a Geranium like a Sultana – and when the Humming birds come down – Geranium and I shut our eyes – and go far away."

🌿 Nasturtiums run rampant in late summer heat.

Flowering vines are the acrobats of any summer garden including Dickinson's, stretching out and scaling heights. Tendrils on sweet peas twist, clinging to string or trellis. "I write in the midst of Sweet-Peas and by the side of Orioles," Dickinson observed, "and could put my Hand on a Butterfly, only he withdraws." Their sweet, fragrant flowers are good for cutting.

Morning glories open to trumpet in the day, silent, unlike the family rooster. "Such a purple morning," Dickinson wrote, "even to the morning-glory that climbs the cherry tree." In an early poem, she employed the ephemeral morning glory as simile and mimicked the style of Robert Burns:

Poor little Heart!
Did they forget thee?
Then dinna care! Then dinna care!

Proud little Heart!
Did they forsake thee?
Be debonair! Be debonair!

Frail little Heart!
I would not break thee -
Could'st credit *me*? Could'st credit me?

Gay little Heart!
Like Morning Glory!
Wind and Sun - wilt thee array!

214, 1861

Like most good gardeners, the Dickinsons shared their yield of produce and received contributions in turn. Dickinson wrote to her cousin Loo one summer, "I cooked the peaches as you told me, and they swelled to beautiful fleshy halves and tasted quite magic." Both peaches and beans were a boon, as she and Vinnie were nursing their aging mother. "The beans we fricasseed and they made a savory cream in cooking that 'Aunt Emily' liked to sip. She was always fonder of julep food than of more substantial." The fruits of the season were appreciated in sickness and health.

In the center of summer, the berries bear fruit. In their younger

🌿 Blackberries "for the parching," as painted by Helen Sharp

years, the Dickinson sisters went berrying with friends, picking raspberries and blackberries that grew in abundance in hedgerows around town. One poem includes berries with alternative medicines, both real and imagined:

> Would you like Summer? Taste of our's -
> Spices? Buy - here!
> Ill! We have Berries, for the parching!
> Weary! Furloughs of Down!
> Perplexed! Estates of Violet - Trouble ne'er looked on!
> Captive! We bring Reprieve of Roses!
> Fainting! Flasks of Air!
> Even for Death - a Fairy Medicine -
> But, which is it - Sir?
>
> 272, 1862

The currant bushes in the Dickinson garden are prolific. A July entry in Vinnie's diary reveals a farmer's early start. "Picked currants at four in morning. Made wine." Sister Emily evidently assisted, as she bragged to Austin the following week that the resulting wine would suit him. Their mother's cookbook included a recipe for fermenting currant wine intended for "those who have more currants than they have money." The wine, in turn, became an ingredient. To a friend Dickinson quipped, "I shall make Wine Jelly Tonight and send you a Tumbler in the Letter, if the Letter consents, a Fabric sometimes obdurate." (Wine jellies were a sort of nineteenth-century homemade Jell-O.)

After supper is a perfect time for an evening constitutional in the garden. A pregnant moon emerges from the dusk, and the flowers become phosphorescent. Pale flowers glow and release copious scent. They attract night pollinators—moths fly at night, resting with open wings on fragrant flowers like four o'clocks. Fireflies blink, candles in the window of a summer night. Bats swoop. Owls hoot. Moth, firefly, bat, owl—Dickinson used all of them as subjects for poems.

As summer progresses, so does the nocturnal decibel level in the garden, the crickets and cicadas joining in percussion and ostinato. But it is strangely soothing, white noise for sleep, an "unobtrusive Mass."

Further in Summer than the Birds -
Pathetic from the Grass -
A minor Nation celebrates
It's unobtrusive Mass -

No Ordinance be seen -
So gradual the Grace
A pensive Custom it becomes
Enlarging Loneliness -

Antiquest felt at Noon -
When August burning low
Arise this spectral Canticle
Repose to typify -

Remit as yet no Grace -
No Furrow on the Glow,
Yet a Druidic Difference
Enhances Nature now -

895, 1865

One morning in September, the air turns crisp, like cotton sheets hanging on the clothesline. The garden steps up to the threshold of autumn.

Autumn

A GARDENER'S TOWN

IN THE 1860s, Emily Dickinson's eyesight began to fail. As writer, reader, and gardener, it must have been terrifying. Recent biographers conclude that it was a condition called iritis, adhesions of the iris and lens that cause pain and extreme sensitivity to light. The affliction was intense enough to rouse her from her habit of seclusion.

She left for Cambridge for two protracted stays in a boarding house with Fanny and Loo, taking regular treatments with an eye doctor. She was a refugee, missing home but making steady progress. To Sue, she sighed, "It would be best to see you – it would be good to see the Grass, and hear the Wind blow the wide way in the Orchard – Are the Apples ripe – Have the Wild Geese crossed – Did you save the seed to the pond Lily?" It was as if she was a continent away.

With the condition stabilized, she came home and wrote back to Loo, "For the first few weeks I did nothing but comfort my plants, till now their small green cheeks are covered with smiles." The care lavished on plants can offer its own brand of healing. For Dickinson it was a balm.

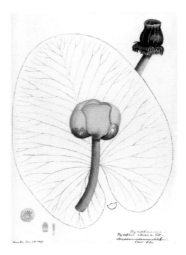

⚘ The cow lily or spatterdock is one of the aquatic lilies local to Amherst. Painting by Helen Sharp.

🪶 The train curved passed Amherst College and alongside the
Hills Hat Factory, south of the Dickinson meadow. In the 1860s,
the New London Northern Railroad acquired the line.

The Amherst she returned to was a vibrant place. From her growing up years the townscape had progressed. Thanks in good measure to her father's efforts, the Amherst and Belchertown Railroad had come to town in the 1850s, crossing Main Street to the east of the Homestead, tethering Amherst to the larger world by a new umbilical.

Since her grandfather's time, Amherst had balanced between town and gown, and so did the Dickinsons. Edward Dickinson, longtime treasurer of Amherst College, upheld a tradition of an annual open house for the senior class, their professors, and local gentry. The guests would have spilled out into the garden, discussing religion, politics, and war news. Emily continued to help her family host these events, serving wine, tea, and conversation, well after she stopped going out into society.

If town was expanding, gown was also putting on new growth. Amherst College continued its building program: adding, expanding, and updating its quarters. Frederick Law Olmsted wrote a report on the college landscape for Austin and his fellow trustees. Olmsted conferred on the institution an appreciation of the mountain view west from the crest of the campus.

At Austin's request, Olmsted also advised on improvements around the town proper. The Dickinson law offices looked out onto Amherst's town common. It was partly a swamp in those days; one area was something of a frog pond. Olmsted submitted a sketch with a wide semicircle of trees for the public space. While his design was never implemented per se, Austin Dickinson and his neighbors accomplished their tree planting program in a most Victorian way—by forming a village improvement society. On October 5, 1857, Austin and a group of like-minded gentlemen from town formed the Amherst Ornamental Tree Association. With his legal training, Austin was well-suited to serve on the executive committee and to draft the association's mission:

COLLEGES AND OBSERVATORY AT AMHERST, MASSACHUSETTS.

Amherst College, a passion of three generations of Dickinsons.

> *The laying out and ornamenting the public common, the general improvement and adornment of the various public walks throughout the village by grading, graveling and lining with trees where there are deficiencies, and to do anything which may render the public grounds and ways of our village more attractive and beautiful.*

Trees were for the good of the town. Amherst's central common was flanked with churches and an assortment of buildings—Boltwood's Tavern, a general store, the Amherst House, and brick commercial blocks with shops on the ground floor and offices above. The downtown streets that Emily patronized in her youth had wide sidewalks with railings to hitch horses. As early as 1840, engravings of the town center show regularly spaced street trees. Some early town planner had planted them in front of the retail establishments. The Amherst Ornamental Tree Association followed suit.

Austin would drive out in his carriage with hired men following in a wagon. Sometimes the children went along for the ride. They surveyed

Street tree planting in downtown Amherst in the 1840s included tree guards to protect the saplings.

wild areas in the surrounding countryside, Austin identifying plants and the men digging up saplings and small shrubs— mountain laurels, white pines, small oaks. In wet areas near the forest edge they found white dogwood and pink azalea. Back to town they came, bringing back their horticultural loot. The plants were native to the area, which meant that they were, by definition, hardy and likely to thrive. Mattie remembered, "I loved the part in *Macbeth* where 'Birnam wood do come to Dunsinane.' Hadn't I seen Pelham woods come to Amherst many a time?"

It seems a shame that Emily Dickinson didn't get to witness this gathering of trees, but it was likely that she was able to share in some ways. Period photographs suggest that some of Austin's street trees were planted in front of the Homestead. Then, as now, it pays to be related to someone on the Tree Association. And there is a much-told story of her brother enticing her to the edge of The Evergreens property one evening to see the work he had done landscaping the new Congregational church across the street. Austin created some controversy with his first gambit into ecclesiastical landscape design. One of the more conservative fellow parishioners threatened to quit the parish over the curved approach to the church door. "Not to walk straight up to the Throne of Grace was silly and heathenish—if it was not Papish— or worse." But Austin Dickinson's design advice held sway in the end.

In addition to beautification efforts around town, some of the enterprising citizens of Amherst decided that a water cure could draw more visitors. The springs in Pelham Hill two miles east of town, long a destination for locals—including Emily Dickinson who had collected arbutus there—became the site for a new hotel in 1860.

One year later, on July 6, 1861, the *Springfield Republican* reported on the one-year anniversary of the health resort. There were patriotic songs, a brass band, poems, and—of course—oration. "Speeches were made at the crowded dinner tables by Dr. Stearns, Dr. Hitchcock, and other officers of the college, Edward Dickinson and other gentlemen . . . Dr. Hitchcock during his remarks gave the name of 'Hygean' to the mountain and springs, and christened the hotel the 'Orient.'"

The resort's waters arrived at the Dickinson garden, at least figuratively. One autumn Emily wrote of her sultans, *Impatiens walleriana*, "Aunt Katie and the Sultans have left the Garden now, and parting with my own, recalls their sweet companionship - Mine were not, I think, as exuberant as in other years, - Perhaps the Pelham Water shocked their stately tastes." Dickinson was familiar with the efficacious properties attributed to the water, whether factual or facetious.

Another magnet that brought people to town was the annual Cattle Show, hosted by the East Hampshire Agricultural Society. Edward Dickinson, his neighbor Luke Sweetser, and other like-minded gentleman farmers founded the society on the first of May 1850 "for the encouragement of Agriculture and Mechanic Arts by Premiums and other means in the town of Amherst." Its major event each year was the Cattle Show. Austin once wrote in a letter, "I think too, that Cattle Show day is the pleasantest in the whole year for Amherst. It seems a holiday especially for *Amherst people*, and not a lot of old women and ministers and students and the relatives and stuck up trustees, as Commencement is." He was right, if a bit unkind.

"Cattle Show day is the pleasantest in the whole year for Amherst."

An early morning artillery blast opened the event. Farmers came into town like agricultural Noahs, leading cows, pigs, sheep, horses, and bulls, bleating and whinnying, lowing and stamping. The ladies of town vied with baked goods, preserves, and fancy work. As refinement became more fashionable, fine arts and flower arranging were added. Locals took sides on tractor pulls, likely with some surreptitious wagers changing hands. Sometimes the Belchertown coronet band played.

The Show is not the Show
But they that go -
Menagerie to me
My Neighbor be -
Fair Play -
Both went to see -

1270, 1872

As with any good county fair, the spirit of competition ran high. The Dickinsons took part—they judged and were judged. In 1858, for example, Austin chaired the fine arts category, his mother was a flower judge, and his father judged the carriage horses. Mrs. Dickinson entered her figs, Emily her bread, Susan her flowers. The local paper reported, "a basket and a vase of flowers were at once recognized by some of the Committee, as from the splendid garden of Mrs. W. A. Dickinson, whose diligence and success in the cultivation of flowers is only equaled by her surpassing skill in arranging them." Susan won fifty cents.

Even when the Dickinson sisters chose to stay at home, they were not forgotten. "Austin and Sue have just returned from the Belchertown Cattle Show," Emily reported, "Austin bought me a Balloon and Vinnie a Watermelon."

Nine years later, Susan was judging the floral classes for the Eighteenth Annual Show. In 1867 on September 24th and 25th at Hampshire Park, Susan and the committee awarded prizes to the best arrangements, selections of wild flowers, and collections of garden flowers including dahlias. Professor William S. Clark from Amherst College headed the committee.

Professor Clark was in the midst of a career change. A new college came to town, and Clark became its president. The Morrill Act, passed by Congress in 1862, had specified land be put aside in each state for an agricultural school. Massachusetts chose Amherst for its location the following year. Edward Dickinson, then state senator, lobbied for the location and appropriations for the new "land grant" college. The first class was in session at the Massachusetts Agricultural College by the end of 1867, on farmland north of the town center.

🌿 The Durfee Plant House and its surrounding garden in its early years, with instructor and students from the Massachusetts Agricultural College posing out front.

The campus boasted an ornate glasshouse, the Durfee Plant House, a maharajah's tent in glass, complete with fernery and fishpond. The conservatory and botanic garden were pleasant destinations for an afternoon drive. Designed by Frederick Lord (later of the well-known Lord & Burnham greenhouse firm), it was completed at the end of 1867, thirteen years after Mr. Dickinson had added the conservatory on to the Homestead. Mattie described the Durfee Plant House as "Aunt Emily's conservatory multiplied ever so many times." There was a palm house, a camellia collection, and the "Victoria room" with an aquatic pool starring the giant Amazon waterlily, named *Victoria regia* (later renamed *Victoria amazonica*) in the queen's honor.

The proprietors of the Plant House bestowed cut flowers on visitors. Quantities of stems could also be had for a small price. Susan Dickinson availed herself of their inventory for her arrangements. The Massachusetts Agricultural College also sold ornamental plants for indoors and for garden bedding, as well as vegetables, shrubs, and trees. The offerings were extensive. Their catalog from the 1870s listed fifty varieties of geraniums and sixty named rose cultivars for sale. While it is unlikely that Emily Dickinson visited there during her reclusive years, she would have heard about it from friends and family and read about it in the weekly paper. Sad really, as it would have been a delightful place for her to frequent each year as the growing season waned.

Autumn in Emily Dickinson's Garden

> "We go to sleep with the Peach in our Hands and wake with the Stone, but the Stone is the pledge of Summers to come."

THE SUMMER, which had stretched on like the slow section of a sonata, builds to a crescendo before the launch of an allegro movement. "*Summer*? My memory flutters – had – was there a summer?" Dickinson wrote, "You should have seen the fields go – gay entomology! Swift little ornithology! Dancer, and floor, and cadence quite gathered away, and I, a phantom, rehearse the story! An orator of feather unto an audience of fuzz, – and pantomimic plaudits. 'Quite as good as a play,' indeed!"

❧ "Autumn begins to be inferred."

Summer begins to have the look
Peruser of enchanting Book
Reluctantly but sure perceives
A gain upon the backward leaves

Autumn begins to be inferred
By millinery of the cloud
Or deeper color in the shawl
That wraps the everlasting hill

The eye begins it's avarice
A meditation chastens speech
Some Dyer of a distant tree
Resumes his gaudy industry

Conclusion is the course of all
Almost to be perennial
And then elude stability
Recalls to immortality -

1693, undated

Autumn in New England has earned its reputation. From her bedroom window Emily Dickinson could see the trees assume a new palette. The season is fair-haired. Elm leaves turn gold and drop. In two early letters, Dickinson used Shakespeare's "the sere, the yellow leaf" to describe the gilding. The season is a siren, turning maples and sassafras leaves to wine and rust.

The name - of it - is "Autumn" -
The hue - of it - is Blood -
An Artery - opon the Hill -
A Vein - along the Road -

Great Globules - in the Alleys -
And Oh, the Shower of Stain -
When Winds - upset the Basin -
And spill the Scarlet Rain -

It sprinkles Bonnets - far below -
It gathers ruddy Pools -
Then - eddies like a Rose - away -
Opon Vermilion Wheels -

465, 1862

    With shorter days and cooler nights, the leaves age and physically senesce. Green chlorophyll starts to dissipate, the way a grandparent's skin thins over time. The latent yellows and oranges show through, the color chemistry of bananas and carrots. Leafy sugars are

Maple leaves enhanced by "Some Dyer of a distant tree." Painting by Orra White Hitchcock.

❦ ABOVE Sassafras gathered in "ruddy Pools," painted with a maple leaf, by Orra White Hitchcock.

❦ ABOVE RIGHT Dickinson collected a young sprig of sassafras and mounted it in the herbarium (second row, far right).

❦ RIGHT The white oak reddens in autumn.

triggered to spin new colors like red. The brightest displays come from dry weather and hold until heavy frost. Eventually the cellular glue weakens to break the bond between stem and plant. The leaves abdicate and fly in Dickinson's "Vermilion Wheels."

Small cyclones stir up dried leaves, rifling them like pages in a book. Humidity evaporates, uncovering blue skies. There is a certain smell in the air: dry leaves, wood smoke, with an undertone of crispness.

Walking down the flagstone path in the garden, Dickinson noted, "We are by September and yet my flowers are bold as June." A strange thing happens when the weather cools in fall. Given a reprieve from the heat, the garden comes out of its August doldrums to have a second flush of bloom. "There is not yet Frost, and Vinnie's Garden from the door looks like a Pond, with Sunset on it. Bathing in that heals her. How simple is Bethesda!" she wrote, alluding to the mental and physical consolations of the garden.

Summer has two Beginnings -
Beginning once in June -
Beginning in October
Affectingly again -

Without, perhaps the Riot
But graphicker for Grace -
As finer is a going
Than a remaining Face -
Departing then - forever -
Forever - until May -
Forever is deciduous -
Except to those who die -

1457, 1877

The remaining faces in her garden include chrysanthemums, late daisies, and asters. One September, Dickinson wrote in pretend dialogue to Sue, "Evenings get longer with the Autumn – that is nothing new! The Asters are pretty well. 'How are other blossoms?' 'Pretty well, I thank you.'"

Clematis vines twine up their supports with petioles, the short but strong stalks that attach the leaves to the main stems. Some varieties bloom in autumn, and to an observant poet, clematis seeds are irresistible.

Tis Customary as we part
A Trinket - to confer -
It helps to stimulate the faith
When Lovers be afar -

'Tis various - as the various taste -
Clematis - journeying far -
Presents me with a single Curl
Of her Electric Hair -

628, 1863

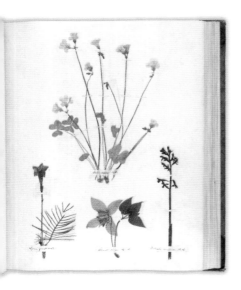

Early autumn signals remontant, or repeat-flowering, roses to push out a few more buds, as if turning their back on the seasonal change. Emily Dickinson sent her cousin a late bloom along with a note that their house-keeper, Maggie Maher, had "'dragged' the garden for this bud for you. You have heard of the 'last rose of summer.' This is that rose's son." Everyone would have known "The Last Rose of Summer," a popular song and one that Dickinson not only played but included in her bound collection of sheet music.

Maggie wasn't the only member of the Dickinson staff who worked in the garden. Describing the vegetables at the North Pleasant Street house, Dickinson had written her brother, "The garden is amazing – we have beets and beans, have had *splendid potatoes* for

⚘ ABOVE LEFT Clematis is bottom center on this herbarium page, though without its electric curl of seeds.

⚘ LEFT Dickinson understood the meaning of the "last rose of summer" both in the garden and sitting at the piano.

three weeks now." Acknowledging their gardener in an offhand way, she continued, "Old Amos weeds and hoes and has oversight of all thoughtless vegetables."

Many hired men helped in the Dickinson gardens, first at North Pleasant Street and later at Main. Gentlemen like Edward and Austin Dickinson lacked the time and had the money to pay for the heavy work to be done. Horace Church gardened for many years both for the family and for Amherst College. A young Emily remembered him:

> *He is the one who spoke patronizingly of the Years, of Trees he sowed in '26,' or Frosts he met in '20,' and was so legendary that it seems like the death of the College Tower, our first Antiquity – I remember he was at one time disinclined to gather the Winter Vegetables till they had frozen, and when Father demurred, he replied 'Squire, ef the Frost is the Lord's Will, I dont popose to stan in the way of it.'*

The harvest was an outward and visible sign of the Lord's will and the hard work of all who had attended it.

The vegetables at the Homestead occupy a large plot beyond the flower garden, separated visually by an asparagus bed. Asparagus stalks shoot up from the roots in early spring, giving the family fresh cuttings that will last almost two months. By foregoing the thinner stems, the bed builds up strength for the following year. Left to their own devices, those pencil thin stems burst into a bank of rich ferny foliage. Later in the year vases of asparagus fronds decorate the stoves and fireplaces in the house. Asparagus is a crossover plant, both functional and decorative, perfectly suited to divide the flowers from their productive, if more pedestrian, neighbors

Beyond the asparagus bed, pole beans twine up stakes, "flaunted red and white, like country girls in gay calico," as Mattie described them. These colorful climbers are scarlet runner beans. They grow next to rows of lima beans and tall, tasseled corn.

While flowers appear in force and fruit on occasion, vegetables rarely made it into Dickinson's poems. But in one, she suggested that raising corn or grapes (or poetry) in New England soil wasn't easy.

On the Bleakness of my Lot
Bloom I strove to raise -
Late - my Garden of a Rock
Yielded Grape - and Maise -

From 862, 1864

The Dickinson vegetable garden was planned and planted with winter in mind, featuring selections that would hold until the spring. Dickinson joked with one correspondent, "Gentlemen here have a way of plucking the tops of trees, and putting the fields in their cellars annually, which in point of taste is execrable, and would they please omit, I should have fine vegetation & foliage all the year round, and never a winter month."

Winter squashes grow on great sprawling plants. Mattie remembered that their vines "trailed over everything the summer left behind right up to frost." In order to keep properly, the squash have to stay on their vines until they are mature. Once the vines wilt, the fruit is ripe and ready to be cut. When dried and stored with care, the rinds are tough and the inner fruit stays firm.

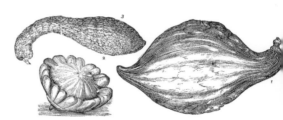

❋ Whether Hubbard or pattypan or crooked neck is unknown, but the Dickinsons grew some varieties of hard winter squash.

There are cabbages and celery in ranks. Both appreciate cooler weather. The cabbages form great globes surrounded by halos of looser leaves. Thanks to Mattie, we know that there were at least two cabbage varieties at the Homestead, green and purple. Celery grows in trenches like rows of toy soldiers, six or eight inches apart, making them easier to manage. The plants are banked up with soil as they grow. By autumn only the top leaves show, blanching

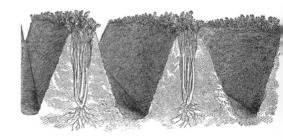

❋ The Dickinsons' gardeners banked up the celery for winter.

the stalks for sweetness and tenderness. Banking celery in this way also puts them in the virtual bank, since it makes a mini-root cellar for each plant and holds it past frost.

> The Products of my Farm are these
> Sufficient for my Own
> And here and there a Benefit
> Unto a Neighbor's Bin.
>
> With us, 'tis Harvest all the Year
> For when the Frosts begin
> We just reverse the Zodiac
> And fetch the Acres in -
>
> 1036, 1865

When the frost begins, the cellar fills. Root vegetables are a favorite. The beets blaze in the garden, "How the sun shone through the beet leaves as through a glass of Burgundy, setting their red veins on fire!" wrote Mattie. When Edward Dickinson was in Congress, he sent back turnip seed from the Patent Office to Horace Church, instructing, "Let Horace save it, somewhere, for winter turnips." The turnips might have been used to feed the livestock.

The harvest is not limited to the cultivated garden. Nuts bounce to the ground, animating the season in an orgy of seed dispersal before winter dormancy. Acorns from the Homestead's white oak thump down, ready for harvest by the squirrels.

> A Saucer holds a Cup
> In sordid human Life
> But in a Squirrel's estimate
> A Saucer holds a Loaf -
>
> A Table of a Tree
> Demands the little King
> And every Breeze that run along
> His Dining Room do swing -

His Cutlery - he keeps
Within his Russet Lips -
To see it flashing when he dines
Do Birmingham eclipse -

Convicted - could we be
Of our Minutiae
The smallest Citizen that flies
Is heartier than we -

1407, 1876

There are nuts for human consumption as well. Black walnuts fall, sheathed in thick green skins. They need to be carefully dried and peeled before cracking. Hickories are another tough nut, needing a heavy hand and a heavier hammer. The chestnuts are ripe, splitting their burrs.

A younger Emily went "chestnuting" on outings with family and friends. Roasting chestnuts yields succulent flesh, a taste specific to the season. To describe herself, Dickinson once wrote, "I am small, like the Wren, and my Hair is bold, like the Chestnut Bur – and my eyes, like the Sherry in the Glass, that the Guest leaves."

The chestnuts also made convenient chronometers. "I havn't felt quite as well as usual since the Chestnuts were ripe, though it was'nt the Chestnuts' fault," Dickinson reported. Other members of the plant kingdom acted as clock substitutes. She once wrote to her friend, Samuel Bowles, "We reckon – your coming by the Fruit. When the Grape gets by – and the Pippin, and the Chestnut – when the Days are a little short by the clock – and a little long by the want – when the sky has new Red Gowns – and a Purple Bonnet."

She could easily reckon time by the grapes since their trellises stood in front of the barn. Another October, she had described their realm to Austin, "The grapes too are fine, juicy, and such a purple – I fancy the robes of kings are not a tint more royal. The vine looks like a kingdom, with ripe round grapes for subjects – the first instance on record of subjects devouring kings!" By October, the grapes hang down from their supports, a fable of Aesop ripening in full sun.

Fig trees grow on the opposite side of the grape arbor, getting reflected heat off the barn and shelter from the prevailing winds. Their leaves are arabesques, their branches prolific. Suited to Mediterranean rather than Massachusetts winters, Mrs. Dickinson's figs required elaborate protection, covering or burying the branches to protect their fruit-bearing buds. In Amherst, they were newsworthy. The editor of the local gazette reported receiving a basket of fresh figs, a press release of ripe fruit. If a garden is a reflection of the gardener, what do fig trees tell of Emily Norcross Dickinson? Perhaps Dickinson's mother accepted a challenge and savored the curious, the unusual.

✿ Emily Norcross Dickinson was proud of her figs.

The orchard appears over and over again in Dickinson's poems.

The Robin's my Criterion for Tune -
Because I grow - where Robins do -
But, were I Cuckoo born -
I'd swear by him -
The ode familiar - rules the Noon -
The Buttercup's, my Whim for Bloom -
Because, we're Orchard sprung -
But, were I Britain born,
I'd Daisies spurn -

None but the Nut - October fit -
Because - through dropping it,
The Seasons flit - I'm taught -
Without the Snow's Tableau
Winter, were lie - to me -
Because I see - New Englandly -
The Queen, discerns like me -
Provincially -

256, 1861

A robin finds a handy perch on a tool handle in the Homestead garden.

A SELECTION OF
EMILY DICKINSON'S
Apples

❧ The young trees will grow to recreate the Dickinson orchard.

❧ BELOW Lavinia Dickinson preferred Baldwins. Painting by Helen Sharp.

GOLDEN SWEET. They are, of course, yellow apples, large and pale. In the Dickinson orchard, they were even sweeter because of the nostalgia. "The Aunt that has shared her Blossoms with me, must have a cluster of mine." Dickinson wrote, "The Golden Sweets are from Grandfather's Tree."

RUSSET. The russets are rough, their surfaces reminding someone of the homespun cloth that is their namesake. Mr. Dickinson would have called them "good keepers." Put in the cellar in November, they will keep until June. In point of fact they're not the tastiest apples, but if you wanted an apple pie in the spring in nineteenth-century Amherst, russets were welcome regardless of their faults.

> It is an honorable Thought
> And make One lift One's Hat
> As One met sudden Gentlefolk
> Opon a daily Street
>
> That We've immortal Place
> Though Pyramids decay
> And Kingdoms, like the Orchard
> Flit Russetly away
>
> 1115, 1865

BALDWIN. Bright red, crisp, and juicy, Baldwin apples originated in eastern Massachusetts from a chance seedling. They are prolific. "We have no Fruit this year, the Frost having barreled that in the Bud – except the 'Fruits of the Spirit,' but Vinnie prefers Baldwins." In "Fruits of the Spirit" Dickinson was quoting Galatians.

In his library, Mr. Dickinson paged through a small volume called *The Fruit Garden* by Patrick Barry. Mr. Barry, of the Mount Hope Nursery in Rochester, New York, connected good morals, patriotism, and the cultivation of fruit in a way that must have pleased Edward Dickinson:

> *Aside from the beneficial results to individual and public health and prosperity from this general union of the fruit garden and the dwelling, it cannot fail to exercise a softening and refining influence on the tastes, habits, and manners of the people, and greatly strengthen their love of home and country.*

Small wonder that the Dickinsons appreciated their fruit garden, especially the apples.

The apples from the Dickinson orchard were the source of another staple for the table—cider, both fresh and fermented. There is some evidence of a cider house on the property, or they may have taken their apples to a local cider press. A young Emily once enthused, "The cider is almost done – we shall have some I guess by Saturday, at *any rate by Sunday noon!*"

In the Dickinson autumn orchard, apples ripen and fall, opportunities for commentary on workers and wildlife. "Men are picking up the apples to-day, and the pretty boarders are leaving the trees, birds and ants and bees," wrote Dickinson. "I have heard a chipper say 'dee' six times in disapprobation. How should we like to have our privileges wheeled away in a barrel?"

In addition to apples, the orchard includes peaches, pears, plums, and quinces. Dickinson

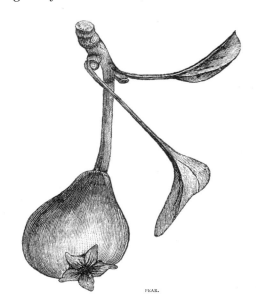

PEAR.

✣ "Hips like hams, and the flesh of bonbons."

captured their merits in her correspondence. Her description of sugar pears is luscious, "hips like hams, and the flesh of bonbons." To one friend, she was effervescent, "It was so delicious to see you – a Peach before the time, it makes all seasons possible and Zones – a caprice." To another, she penned an admonition against addressing joint correspondence to her and Vinnie, "A mutual plum is not a plum. I was too respectful to take the pulp and do not like the stone." And at least one quince must have grown on the Dickinson property as Mrs. Jameson, a neighbor, told her son, "Vinnie sent me over some lovely quinces yesterday so I shall have something nice for the winter."

Besides the autumn poets sing
A few prosaic days
A little this side of the snow
And that side of the Haze -

A few incisive mornings -
A few Ascetic eves -
Gone - Mr. Bryant's "Golden Rod"
And Mr. Thomson's "Sheaves."

Still, is the bustle in the brook -
Sealed are the spicy valves -
Mesmeric fingers softly touch
The eyes of many Elves -

Perhaps a squirrel may remain -
My sentiments to share -
Grant me, O Lord, a sunny mind -
Thy windy will to bear!

123, 1859

The season can't seem to make up its mind, with the teasing warmth of Indian summer interludes. Alert gardeners watch for a day of just the right temperature to dig up plants from the flowerbeds and move the potted plants indoors. It is a balancing act. "The plants went into camp last night," Dickinson wrote one autumn morning, "their tender armor insufficient for the crafty nights." The camp for her plants was the conservatory.

These are the days when Birds come back -
A very few - a Bird or two -
To take a backward look.

These are the days when skies resume
The old - old sophistries of June -
A blue and gold mistake.

Oh fraud that cannot cheat the Bee.
Almost thy plausibility
Induces my belief,

Till ranks of seeds their witness bear -
And softly thro' the altered air
Hurries a timid leaf.

Oh sacrament of summer days,
Oh Last Communion in the Haze -
Permit a child to join -

Thy sacred emblems to partake -
Thy consecrated bread to take
And thine immortal wine!

122, 1859

In the Dickinson meadow, the goldenrod is yellow, the asters purple. Bees gather nectar and pollen into hives, building winter stores. In the hills around Amherst the gentians bloom a bright purple-blue, like pigment straight from a tube of paint.

God made a little Gentian -
It tried - to be a Rose -
And failed - and all the Summer laughed -
But just before the Snows

There rose a Purple Creature -
That ravished all the Hill -
And Summer hid her Forehead -
And Mockery - was still -

The Frosts were her condition -
The Tyrian would not come
Until the North - invoke it -
Creator - Shall I - bloom?

520, 1863

("Tyrian" was the purple dye used for the togas of Roman emperors.)

In the margins of the woodland, witch hazel lets down its yellow hair. Witch hazel, *Hamamelis virginiana*, is a large shrub inhabiting the understory around Amherst. Dickinson described it best, calling it "a lovely alien." When Fanny and Loo sent her a sprig, Emily elaborated. "It looked like tinsel fringe combined with staider fringes, witch and witching too, to my joyful mind," she wrote. "Is there not a dim suggestion of a dandelion, if her hair were raveled and she grew on a twig instead of a tube, – though this is timidly submitted." It does have that otherworldly look. She once said of witch hazel, "It haunted me like child-hood's Indian pipe, or ecstatic puff-balls, or that mysterious apple that sometimes comes on river-pinks."

🌿 The bright yellow leaves and "lovely alien" blooms of fall-blooming witch hazel, in a painting by Helen Sharp.

Some plants come to the gardener, rather than the other way around. And autumn is a season for hitchhiker seeds.

A Burdock - twitched my Gown -
Not Burdock's blame - but mine
Who went too near the Burdock's Den -

A Bog - affronts my shoe.
What else have Bogs to do -
The only Trade they know -
The splashing Men?

'Tis Minnows - should despise -
An Elephant's calm eyes
Look further on.

289, 1862

The first frost can descend on Amherst before October, only five months from the last frost in May. Dickinson once wrote, "In early Autumn we had Mid-winter Frost – 'When God is with us, who shall be against us,' but when he is against us, other allies are useless." The frost is a disturbing lover.

A Visitor in Marl -
Who influences Flowers -
Till they are orderly as Busts -
And Elegant - as Glass -

Who visits in the Night -
And just before the Sun -
Concludes his glistening interview -
Caresses - and is gone -

But whom his fingers touched -
And where his feet have run -

🌿 "A Visitor in Marl" can curtail leaf color, like the red in the dogwood foliage.

And whatsoever Mouth he kissed -
Is as it had not been -

558, 1863

In one letter Dickinson sighed, "Veils of Kamchatka dim the Rose, in my Puritan garden." In another, she mourned, "I trust your Garden was willing to die – I do not think that mine was – it perished with beautiful reluctance, like an Evening Star." Autumn's end is stark, the trees bare and the ground exposed. Emily Dickinson dreamed of leap-frogging the winter to the spring that would follow.

We should not mind so small a flower -
Except it quiet bring
Our little garden that we lost
Back to the Lawn again.

So spicy her Carnations nod -
So drunken reel her Bees -
So silver steal a hundred flutes
From out a hundred trees -

That whoso sees this little flower
By faith may clear behold
The Bobolinks around the throne
And Dandelions gold.

82, 1859

Winter is, however, inevitable.

Winter

REQUIEM FOR A GARDENER

THE LAST YEARS OF EMILY DICKINSON'S LIFE were a winter of loss. As she physically removed herself from the wider world, death increased its visits to her intimates. In eleven years she lost six key people from her personal orbit, beginning in 1874 with her father. Edward Dickinson died suddenly that year, leaving the Dickinson women behind at the Homestead. She missed her father in a litany of ways, both routine and immense: the bread she baked for him in particular, the gravitational pull he exerted from the moment he walked through the door, the plants he bought for her garden. She was forty-three years old.

There's a certain Slant of light,
Winter Afternoons -
That oppresses, like the Heft
Of Cathedral Tunes -

Heavenly Hurt, it gives us -
We can find no scar,
But internal difference -
Where the Meanings, are -

None may teach it - Any -
'Tis the Seal Despair -
An imperial affliction
Sent us of the Air -

When it comes, the Landscape listens -
Shadows - hold their breath -
When it goes, 'tis like the Distance
On the look of Death -

320, 1862

That winter, she stared out her window at the stark landscape, conjuring her father's memory. She called it an austere afternoon. Describing her grief, she wrote a letter to her friend, Elizabeth Holland, with phrasing and line breaks that had the intensity of a poem: "No event of Wind or Bird breaks the Spell of Steel. Nature squanders Rigor – now – where she squandered Love." She closed her letter with "The Hand that plucked the Clover – I seek."

The following year, her mother suffered a debilitating stroke leaving her bedridden. It seemed to seal Dickinson's reclusiveness. The gardens were still an escape. "I do not go away, but the Grounds are ample – almost travel – to me – and the few that I knew – came – since my Father died." The hemlock hedge surrounding those ample grounds transported her further north to the boreal forests of Scandinavia and the river basins of Russia—the Dnieper and Don.

I think the Hemlock likes to stand
Opon a Marge of Snow -
It suits his own Austerity -
And satisfies an awe

That men, must slake in Wilderness -
And in the Desert - cloy -
An instinct for the Hoar, the Bald -
Lapland's - necessity -

The Hemlock's nature thrives - on cold -
The Gnash of Northern winds
Is sweetest nutriment - to him -
His best Norwegian Wines -

🌿 The homestead in winter, circa 1885, showing the snow-covered hemlocks.

> To satin Races - he is nought -
> But children on the Don,
> Beneath his Tabernacles, play,
> And Dnieper Wrestlers, run.
>
> 400, 1862

Within the house, the two sisters cared for their mother for years. Up and down the stairs they went, bringing her special food or a blossom from the garden. Vinnie wrote of their mother, "She was so fond of every bird & flower & so full of pity for every grief." Emily Norcross Dickinson died on November 14, 1882.

⚘ When Gib died, his family closed his room, preserving his childhood like a time capsule.

The following year came the hardest loss of all, next door at The Evergreens. Eight-year-old Gib, Dickinson's youngest nephew Thomas Gilbert, died of typhoid in the autumn of 1883. Aunt Emily sat by his bed on the night before he died, watching the beloved bright star of the family fade out.

Dickinson went from tending people to tending graves, the small cemetery just a short distance from the house. The two sisters walked up the hill and decorated the graves with flowers during the growing season: lily-of-the-valley for Gib, flowering branches of hawthorn for their parents.

The proximity of death brought thoughts of her own departure. "When it shall come to my turn," Dickinson mused in a letter, "I want a Buttercup – Doubtless the Grass will give me one, for does she not revere the whims of her flitting Children?" All the regrets surfaced, the bittersweet hope of a next life. "I wish, until I tremble, to touch the ones I love before the hills are red – are gray – are white – are 'born again'! If we knew how deep the crocus lay, we never should let her go."

Even with her grief, Emily Dickinson continued to see longtime friends. Her correspondence never ebbed. One example was Helen Hunt Jackson, née Helen Fiske, a childhood friend. Perhaps you remember young Emily playing with Helen under the syringas. Their relationship did not end there.

Both born in Amherst in 1830, Emily and Helen shared interests in gardening and the natural world. And they seemed to have a mutual attachment to mud. Helen's mother once scolded her daughter:

> As to playing in the barn and shed I would rather have you play in the house; and in the garden when it is pleasant, you will make more washing if you are round in such places, the weather is becoming cold, too, and they are not so proper for Misses as within doors and in the garden.

The two girls were schoolmates for a time in the lower grades, and then Emily enrolled in Amherst Academy as a day student while Helen went to boarding school. Helen's letters home from Ipswich Academy discussed her garden with its moss pinks, irises, roses, honeysuckle, and polyanthus. In her teens, after the death of her parents, Helen left Amherst to live with an uncle.

The two women reconnected as adults in 1860 after Helen had married Major Edward Hunt. Dickinson was charmed with the couple, particularly remembering the major saying that "her great dog 'understood gravitation.'" The women continued to exchange letters through the years.

After her husband died, Helen turned to writing professionally—poems, essays, fiction, children's books, a book on wildflowers. She remarried and became, as Helen Hunt Jackson, a well-known literary figure. One of Jackson's novels, *Mercy Philbrick's Choice*, was said by some to draw on Emily Dickinson's life. Scholars today see it as autobiographical. It seems to draw from the lives of both, depicting an Amherst woman with horticultural and literary interests. The main character collects woodland plants:

> *There were three different species of ground-pine in these woods, and hepatica and pyrola and winter-green and thickets of laurel. What wealth for a lover of wild, out-door things! Each day Mercy bore home new treasures, until the house was almost as green and fragrant as a summer wood.*

Mercy's garden seems evocative of Dickinson's, including "the quaint, trim beds of old-fashioned pinks and ladies' delights and sweet-williams which bordered the little path." Emily Dickinson would have been delighted.

Jackson was introduced to Thomas Wentworth Higginson who encouraged her efforts. Learning she hailed originally from Amherst, he showed her some of Dickinson's unusual poems. Jackson saw genius. "You are a great poet," she wrote in a letter to Dickinson, "and it is wrong to the day you live in, that you will not sing aloud. When you are what men call dead, you will be sorry you were so stingy."

Tantalizingly few of their letters survived, but in one that does, Dickinson sent Jackson a poem about a bluebird. Impressed, Jackson replied, "We have blue birds here – I might have had the sense to write about one myself, but I never did: and now I never can." She laid out a tempting proposal at the end of her letter, "What should you think of trying your hand on the oriole? He will be along presently."

Dickinson responded with the poem, "One of the ones that Midas touched," dubbing the oriole "a Pleader," "a Dissembler," "an Epicure," "a Thief." Not to be one-upped, she continued, "To the Oriole you suggested I add a Humming Bird and hope they are not untrue." The hummingbird she added was a tour de force.

A Route of Evanescence,
With a revolving Wheel -
A Resonance of Emerald
A Rush of Cochineal -
And every Blossom on the Bush
Adjusts its tumbled Head -
The mail from Tunis - probably,
An easy Morning's Ride -

1489, 1879

Jackson was ready to promote Dickinson's work. She convinced her to include "Success is counted sweetest" in the *No Name Series*, part of the *Masque of Poets* anthology. She also asked to act as her literary executor. That is, Helen Hunt Jackson would have undertaken the posthumous publication of Dickinson's poems. But it was not to be. Jackson died too soon, in 1885.

❧ A ruby-throated hummingbird resting along its route.

In addition to maintaining ties with old friends, Dickinson made a new friend in her final years. Mabel Loomis Todd made a grand entrance in Amherst, arriving in September 1881 with her husband, David, the new astronomy professor at Amherst College, and their infant daughter, Millicent. Mabel sang and played the piano, wrote,

In this theatrical tableau, Mabel Loomis Todd is standing in the white dress in the center with Susan Dickinson seated next to her, holding Gib and looking toward Mattie, who is wearing a straw hat in front of the fireplace. David Todd is at the far right in a boater hat. Ned Dickinson is stretched out in the front row with a tennis racket.

acted, and painted. She was young. (Mabel was twenty-five years younger than Emily.) With her intelligence, good looks, and accomplishments, she must have seemed phosphorescent to the Dickinson siblings.

Susan immediately recruited the couple as regular dinner guests at The Evergreens. Mabel often visited the Homestead, making conversation with Vinnie, singing and playing the parlor's piano. The older Dickinson sister listened from the hallway or the top of the stairs. After Beethoven or Bach or Scarlatti, a tray would arrive in the parlor—carried by the housekeeper—with a glass of sherry, a poem from Emily, or a flower from her garden to reward the performance.

While the two never met face-to-face, Todd and Dickinson were well-matched with mutual enthusiasm for plants, music, and the written word. Mabel reported in a letter to her parents, "Soon after I came home a box of the most exquisite flowers came for me—hyacinths, heliotrope, and some odd yellow flowers which I do not know—from—who do you imagine? Miss Emily Dickinson!"

Mabel Todd was a skilled botanical artist. In 1882, she sent Dickinson a wooden panel painted with Indian pipes. The painting elicited an enthusiastic response. "That without suspecting it you should send me the preferred flower of life, seems almost supernatural, and the sweet glee that I felt at meeting it, I could confide to none," wrote Dickinson. "I still cherish the clutch with which I bore it from the ground when a wondering Child, an unearthly booty, and maturity only enhances mystery, never decreases it." Indian pipes appear in the herbarium, collected some forty years before.

The Indian pipe (*Monotropa uniflora*) is a curious plant. It looks like a waxy albino stem of lily-of-the-valley, white and leafless. The flowers bend to the ground, a nod to its generic name, *Monotropa*, Greek for "one turn." Native to the Northeast, it is an angiosperm—a flowering plant—but one incapable of photosynthesis. Unlike the usual green growing things, it can't manufacture its own food but relies on symbiotic relationships. Special fungi named mycorrhizae colonize tree roots and send nutrients like nitrogen and phosphorus to larger plants like oaks and conifers. In exchange, the fungi return food from the tree roots to the Indian pipes. It is botanical barter at its best.

One might say that Emily Dickinson was like Indian pipes. She relied on family members, first her father, then Vinnie, for exchanges with the outside world: necessities, protection, and news. Her niece described Aunt Lavinia as "the man of the household." A month after receiving the painted panel, Emily wrote to Mabel, "I cannot make an Indian Pipe but please accept a Humming Bird." As with Helen Hunt Jackson, she included the poem "A Route of Evanescence." She signed her note "E. Dickinson."

After the episode of the Indian pipes, Mabel Todd would be a footnote in the Emily Dickinson annals—if not for two things. First, she and Austin Dickinson became lovers, and second, she unveiled Dickinson's poems to the world.

🌣 Mabel Loomis Todd's Indian pipes.

Austin and Mabel? They seemed an unlikely couple. Both married and twenty-seven years apart in age, it was an autumn-to-spring romance. They first "declared" in 1882, on one of their many long drives around the Amherst countryside.

Their relationship grew in secret but became common knowledge. Nothing like a small town to brew a scandal operatic in proportion. Mabel said of Austin:

> He was as much a poet as [Emily]. Only his genius did not flower in verse or rhyme, but rather in an intense and cultivated knowledge of nature, in a passionate joy in the landscapes to be seen from many a hilltop near Amherst, and in the multitude of trees and blossoming shrubs all about him.

He had excused himself to Mabel one day, driving off to supervise the digging of a tree for installation on the college campus. "I don't like to trust anyone with an oak," he said.

Austin cut a road along the edge of the meadow and helped Mabel and David site and landscape their new home. It was just a block from The Evergreens, and a new path was quickly worn across the meadow. Enthusiastic about a new love, and, one supposes, a new space to garden, he planted. And planted. Trees and shrubs, iris beds, and vegetables. Mabel described his horticultural endeavors at this "most artistic and beautiful" house some years later:

> My own place is now a perfect bower of beauty, with the touch of my beloved on every inch. The splendid blue spruce, the hemlocks, the white birches, forsythia, hydrangeas, magnolia, beech, chestnut, walnut, ginkgo—all the myriad lovely things he put in here are living vigorously, and it is an enchanting little place.

She called her new home "The Dell."

The Dickinson sisters accepted the couple, as did Mabel's husband, David, causing obvious tensions with Austin's wife, Susan. Mutton-chopped Austin and Mabel with her ringlets sometimes met in the Homestead's parlor. Is it too cliché to picture the couple in the conservatory or strolling in the garden with the smell of the honeysuckle wafting over from the trellises? At least they would have

✣ ABOVE The Dickinson meadow from its northeast corner on Main Street, looking across to Amherst College on the hill and Mabel and David Todd's new home with its arched upper porch just to the right of center.

✣ BELOW The Dell in 1894, showing many of the trees planted by Austin Dickinson.

been out of sight of The Evergreens. Their bond lasted. While neither divorced, their connection ended only with Austin's death in 1895.

Emily Dickinson also had intense relationships with men and women throughout her life, though their extents and, at times, identities are obscured. Late in life she had one substantiated love. Otis Phillips Lord, a long-time family friend, was a retired judge of the Massachusetts Supreme Court. Eighteen years her senior, Lord was a staunch Whig like Dickinson's father, and by 1877 a widower. A photograph from 1883 shows him sitting in his garden in Salem.

Thy flower - be gay -
Her Lord - away!
It ill becometh me -
I'll dwell in Calyx - Gray -
How modestly - alway -
Thy Daisy -
Draped for thee!

From 367, 1862

This poem was written earlier than biographers can verify her bond with Lord. Was it tongue in cheek, playing on his surname, or just coincidence? If the latter, Dickinson must have been amused by it.

She and Lord never married, though fragmentary evidence suggests that he proposed and she considered it. His nieces, who lived with him and stood to inherit his money, were opposed. But his failing health decided the question. He died in 1884. As Dickinson had once written, "My House is a House of Snow – true – sadly – of few."

Winter in Emily Dickinson's Garden

Winter under cultivation
Is as arable as Spring

—1720, undated

WINTER IN AMHERST IS DARK. Days abbreviate. On the first day of winter the sun sets around 4:30. In front of the Homestead, Main

Dickinson's "House of Snow."

Street isn't plowed. Snow is packed down and runners replace wheels on the carriages. Sleighs come out of stables and are so quiet they need bells to warn pedestrians. Winter is made of "days of jingling bells," Dickinson wrote, recalling the sledding parties and sleigh rides of her youth. Children skate on the shallow, frozen places across the street in the Dickinson meadow. Clear skies are often striped with icy cirrus feathers. Before storms, clouds gather thick and gray. It smells like snow.

The depth of the season can be measured in snowfall. For much of the winter, Dickinson's garden is snow covered, a moonscape. The snow acts as a cold but life-preserving blanket, preventing the

🌱 A snowy Main Street, Amherst, showing Austin's tree planting efforts. First Congregational Church is on the right and the front of The Evergreens is just visible on the left.

thaw-and-freeze that heaves plants out of the ground and kills tender roots. Snow clings to the trees around the house, glazing them into exquisite confections—there is a reason bakers use words like "icing" and "frosting."

In some storms precipitation is confused, sliding from liquid to solid when the temperature hovers around freezing. Dickinson once called it "winter's silver fracture." Icicles, quick stalactites, form in the eaves of house and barn where water trickles down, tapering to points. On days when the ice melts, standing under the eaves could be a dangerous proposition. Tree branches shimmer in the sun.

🌱 The snow-covered path from The Evergreens, circa 1885.

Winter in Dickinson's garden is a time of trees. The deciduous trees are elegant skeletons, sharp silhouettes against the sky. Their screen of leaves abandoned, they show off their mathematical structures. The branching of oaks is alternate, maples opposite. Pruning cuts show in winter. Branches of fruit trees are regularly lopped off to strengthen the fruit buds or open up the center of the tree, allowing more light for ripening next year's crop. Over time with regular pruning, they become sculptural.

The forms of trees emerge around the Homestead and The Evergreens. Oaks hold up their broad shoulders. The American elms that line Main Street look like vases. Maples are oval. Locusts are sinuous, snaky. In the bare branches, nests are revealed—birds' nests and squirrels' dreys.

Trees with prominent bark get their turn at the podium. Beeches with silver trunks look like elephants. Paper birches with bright white exfoliating bark mock the snow. The bark on the sycamores flakes like old skin, leaving mottled trunks in white and gray and brown. Dickinson mentioned the sycamore in the last stanza of a poem, comparing its brown bark to cinnamon or perhaps myrrh, that biblical gift of the Magi used to anoint the dead.

What care the Dead, for Chanticleer -
What care the Dead for Day?
'Tis late your Sunrise vex their Face -
And Purple Ribaldry - of Morning

Pour as blank on them
As on the Tier of Wall
The Mason builded, yesterday,
And equally as cool -

What care the Dead for Summer
The Solstice had no Sun
Could waste the Snow before their Gate -
And knew One Bird a Tune -

Could thrill their Mortised Ear
Of all the Birds that be -
This One - beloved of Mankind
Henceforward cherished be -

What care the Dead for Winter?
Themselves as easy freeze -
June Noon - as January Night -
As soon the South - her Breeze
Of Sycamore - or Cinnamon -
Deposit in a Stone
And put a Stone to keep it Warm -
Give Spices - unto Men -

624, 1863

Conifers supply the structure or bones of many winter gardens, and Dickinson's is no exception. Their dark needles contrast with white. The hemlocks droop with snow. "My garden is a little knoll with faces under it," Dickinson wrote, "and only the pines sing tunes, now the birds are absent." From her upstairs window, she could hear and see the needled branches of a large white pine. More of them shade the drive and the path between the two houses. She sent this poem about a pine to her friend Samuel Bowles, enclosing a cluster of needles to be sure he could decode it.

A feather from the Whippowil
That everlasting - sings!
Whose galleries - are Sunrise -
Whose Opera - the Springs -
Whose Emerald Nest the Ages spin
Of mellow - murmuring thread -
Whose Beryl Egg, what Schoolboys hunt
In "Recess - " Overhead!

208, 1861

The soft, feathery needles of white pine are bluish green, attached to the wood in little bundles. When the wind blows, the needles vibrate to make the pines sing. Their seed-bearing cones are the color of beryl, a pale, sea-green gem.

Some days high winds sweep the Homestead's property clean of snow. The garden exposed is full of ghosts. Perennials like peonies die to the ground, leaving carapaces of foliage, like snakes shedding skins. Their watery stems solidify in the first freezes, and then desiccate under the winter sun. Gray leaves, hollow stalks, the last burst of inflorescence dry. Left in the garden, remnants of last year's plants insulate the crowns, the growing points gathering strength to reemerge in spring. There is nostalgia in a winter garden, but also hope.

Two examples of the "Beryl Egg" Dickinson described in her poem.

Like Brooms of Steel
The Snow and Wind
Had swept the Winter Street -
The House was hooked
The Sun sent out
Faint Deputies of Heat -
Where rode the Bird
The Silence tied
His ample - plodding Steed
The Apple in the Cellar snug
Was all the one that played.

1241, 1872

The Homestead's cellar holds the sturdy output of the growing season. When Dickinson walked down into the "Cellar snug," she could retrieve the summer's crop in a tangible way. Apples, root vegetables, a jar of preserved fruit. Or, if she carried the key to the wine cellar with her, perhaps a wine—currant wine, or maybe Malmsey, a kind of Madeira that her mother preferred. Between the cellar windows at the front of the house was the cabinet where freshly baked gingerbread cooled. Without refrigeration, except for an icebox with ice cut from the local pond, the Dickinsons relied on their cold, dry hoarding–cellar.

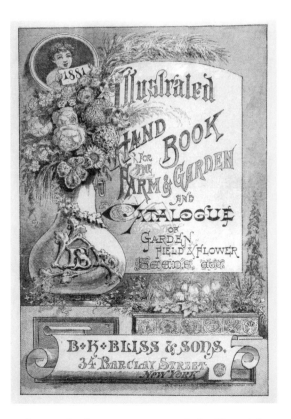

🌿 Prospecting for summer was easy in the Bliss catalog.

Winter is also the season of nursery catalogs, which drift into the mailbox like so much snow. The Dickinsons were not immune to their siren song. In the winter of 1881, Emily described Vinnie "in Bliss' Catalogue, prospecting for Summer."

The Bliss catalog was bliss to any gardener with spring fever that year. It was, in 1881, a weighty book of 141 pages plus supplement. Engravings had that come-hither look, and a full-color chromolithograph of pansies was guaranteed to send any gardener to the order form. The firm of B. K. Bliss—one of America's first mail-order seed houses—was located first in Springfield, Massachusetts, then in New York City. It printed its first catalog with color plates in 1853 and introduced many new varieties of vegetables and flowers into American gardens, including the Dickinson properties on Main Street.

1. GOETHE
2. SCHILLER
3. BEETHOVEN
4. MENDELSOHN

NEW GERMAN PANSIES
From B.K. BLISS & SONS' Gardeners Hand-Book.

5. MOZART
6. HAENDEL
7. HAYDEN
8. SCHUMANN

❧ Perhaps Emily and Vinnie chose some of these pansies from the B. K. Bliss & Sons catalog in the winter of 1881.

Gardeners often favor the rare when shopping catalogs or nurseries. An unusual plant offers bragging rights; there's nothing better than having the first in the neighborhood. In the late 1800s, imports were the latest thing. Austin, for example, planted Norway spruce

(*Picea abies*) at The Evergreens. One of Dickinson's poems describes this manmade movement of plants.

As if some little Arctic flower
Opon the polar hem -
Went wandering down the Latitudes
Until it puzzled came
To continents of summer -
To firmaments of sun -
To strange, bright crowds of flowers -
And birds, of foreign tongue!
I say, As if this little flower
To Eden, wandered in -
What then? Why nothing,
Only, your *inference* therefrom!

177, 1860

Emily Dickinson also prospected for summer with the plants in her conservatory where winter could be "arable as Spring." She described daphne's tiny clusters of sweetly fragrant white flowers as "a more civic Arbutus." Reconsidering she added, "The suggestion is invidious, for are not both as beautiful as Delight can make them?"

Delight also comes from forcing bulbs. In a letter to a friend, Dickinson wrote, "I have made a permanent Rainbow by filling a Window with Hyacinths, which Science will be glad

🌿 A winter view of Spring Street from The Evergreens, showing a Norway spruce.

to know, and have a Cargo of Carnations, worthy of Ceylon." Mattie associated the scent of hyacinths with Aunt Emily's room in winter, "for the way of a bulb in the sunshine had an uncanny fascination for her, their little pots crowding all four window-sills to bring a reluctant spring upon the air." One March, Dickinson wrote to a friend, "I wish I could show you the Hyacinths that embarrass us by their loveliness, though to cower before a flower is perhaps unwise – but Beauty is often timidity – perhaps oftener – pain." There are clandestine pleasures in forcing bulbs. Even though she may have cowered before their beauty, she was never timid about growing them.

As the season wanes, the forecast is changeable. As a girl, Emily enthused, "Haven't we had delightful weather for a week or two? It seems as if Old Winter had forgotten himself. Don't you believe he is absent-minded?" Later in life she described the erratic weather with more mature prose, "It storms in Amherst five days – it snows, and then it rains, and then soft fogs like veils hang on all the houses, and then the days turn Topaz, like a lady's pin." Late winter can be a stubborn season. But as the days stretch into spring, the late snows don't last. Dickinson called them transient.

> Winter is good - his Hoar Delights
> Italic flavor yield -
> To Intellects inebriate
> With Summer, or the World -
>
> Generic as a Quarry
> And hearty - as a Rose -
> Invited with asperity
> But welcome when he goes.
>
> 1374, 1875

Looking out her window, she stood witness to all the seasons in her garden, her "ribbons of the year." Whatever the month, her garden was inspiration for her poems. And her poems have proved perennial indeed.

The Angle of a Landscape -
That every time I wake -
Between my Curtain and the Wall
Opon an ample Crack -

Like a Venetian - waiting -
Accosts my open eye -
Is just a Bough of Apples -
Held slanting, in the Sky -

The Pattern of a Chimney -
The Forehead of a Hill -
Sometimes - a Vane's Forefinger -
But that's - Occasional -

The Seasons - shift - my Picture -
Opon my Emerald Bough,
I wake - to find no - Emeralds
Then - Diamonds - which the Snow

From Polar Caskets - fetched me -
The Chimney - and the Hill -
And just the Steeple's finger -
These - never stir at all -

578, 1863

EMILY DICKINSON DIED ON MAY 15, 1886, at age fifty-six, succumbing
to what the doctor diagnosed as Bright's disease, a kidney ailment.
Her funeral was held in the Homestead's parlor four days later. She
was laid out in a white dress, with violets and a pink lady's slipper
orchid at her throat. Vinnie placed heliotrope by her hand to take to
Judge Lord. Susan arranged violets and ground pine on her white
casket. After the service, the Dickinsons' workmen lifted the casket.
They carried it out from the back of the house and through the garden.

🦋 "The Seasons - shift - my Picture." The Amherst College Special Collections holds this daguerreotype circa 1859 from a private collection. There is strong evidence to support that on the right is Dickinson's friend Kate Scott Turner. Some scholars contend that an adult Emily Dickinson is on the left.

It was a brilliant spring afternoon. Apple blossoms festooned the trees. Mabel Todd remembered, "Then we all walked quietly across the sunny fields, full of innocents & buttercups to the cemetery." She was buried in the family plot with a simple gravestone engraved with her initials, E. E. D. But her story did not end there.

In her final instructions, Dickinson had charged her sister with destroying her papers. Put yourself in Vinnie's shoes. She is sitting in her sister's empty room, perhaps at the well-used writing table. She opens the drawers of the cherry chest and pulls out stacks— decades—of letters from friends and family. Sadly but dutifully, she puts them aside. Later she burns them. But then she finds something amazing—a trove of poems neatly written out in Emily's hand. Thankfully for posterity, Lavinia Dickinson can't bear to get rid of them. There are hundreds and hundreds of poems, including some forty hand-sewn booklets, and many unbound sheets.

Scholars call these booklets "fascicles." Fittingly, *fascicle* is also a botanical term for a cluster of leaves or flowers or roots growing together from a base. Emily Dickinson's work, the careful copying,

Ranunculaceae
Ranunculus . Crowfoot . Buttercup .
R . bulbosus . Bulbous C . or B .

Taunton June 29 '93.

❧ Buttercups bloomed the day of Emily Dickinson's burial. Painting by Helen Sharp.

🌿 Emily Dickinson's gravestone was later replaced by
her niece with this more detailed carving.

ordering, and binding, and her small notations—she put small crosses
with alternate word choices—was like her herbarium, carefully
arranged and bound. "In childhood I never sowed a seed unless it was
perennial – and that is why my garden lasts," Dickinson wrote.

With what Lavinia Dickinson later called her "Joan of Arc feel-
ing," she brought the cache of poems first to her sister-in-law next
door. Susan Dickinson chose to send them out slowly to periodicals.
It was too slow for Vinnie. Recovering them from The Evergreens,
Vinnie marched across Main Street to The Dell, to Mabel Loomis
Todd. In turn, Todd took up the banner, convincing Thomas
Wentworth Higginson that, after all his years of deferment, the poems
were worthy of publication. Todd spent days, hours, years deciphering
the handwritten manuscripts and tracking down Dickinson's letters.
She transcribed the poet's spidery script using an ancient typewriter
to ready them for the typesetters. Mabel Loomis Todd's Indian pipes
graced the front cover of the first edition of Dickinson's poems.

Emily Dickinson had always been ambivalent about publishing.
"Publication - is the Auction / Of the Mind of Man" is the opening to one

of her poems. With a wintry allusion, she continued, "but We - would rather / From Our Garret go / White - Unto the White Creator - / Than invest - Our Snow." She invested her snow—her poems—by depositing them in a cherry chest, waiting for a new season to see them in print.

🌺 The cover of the first edition of Emily Dickinson's poems.

A POET'S GARDENS

Planting a Poet's Garden

EVERY GARDEN IS ANCHORED. It is tied to place—the lay of the land, the composition of the soil. At the Homestead and The Evergreens, they worked sandy loam, a soil formed over eons from the granite that seems to define the New England character. The swales and ridges of the properties whisper of ancient times, echoes of the last glaciation. At roughly the same time, geologically speaking, that humans first crossed the Bering Land Bridge into North America, the land formations around Amherst were settling into their current guise.

To plant a garden like Emily Dickinson's, start with the soil. The Dickinson hired men top-dressed or tilled in amendments: well-rotted manure from stable and barnyard, plus wood ash or wash water from the laundry to "sweeten" the soil with alkali. Perhaps they added store-bought fertilizer. Hastings, a vendor in town, advertised guano and super-phosphate of lime. Emily

Dickinson documented the process of building soil fertility, though she relocated it to an African clime.

Soil of Flint, if steady tilled
Will refund by Hand -
Seed of Palm, by Lybian Sun
Fructified in Sand -

From 862, 1864

To prepared soil, a gardener adds plants. Emily Dickinson had the gift of improvisation in her writing, on the piano keyboard, and in the garden. Unafraid of new combinations of words, musical notes, or flowers, she tried many new plants, sourcing seeds from catalogs like B. K. Bliss. There were local sources too. Mr. Speare, whose shop was just up Main Street at No. 1 Phoenix Row, advertised "Flower Seeds, (Annuals, Bien[n]ials, and Peren[n]ials)" in the local paper. Geneva Nurseries, run by Thomas Judd and his son in South Hadley Falls,

❧ OPPOSITE Orra White Hitchcock's painting of the mountains, hills, and valleys around Amherst.

❧ BELOW Emily Dickinson added plants like campanula to her prepared garden beds.

offered "Flowering Shrubs, Greenhouse Plants, Bulbs &c" in *The Hampshire Express* on May 3, 1866.

To plant an Emily Dickinson garden, a gardener must don a variety of hats including propagator, midwife to Flora. The simple act of planting a seed brings life from dormancy. Dickinson once noted, "How few suggestions germinate," but seeds are simpler than suggestions. She captured the seed at the moment of breaking, the embryo morphing to send radicle down and stem up toward the light.

GERMINATING PLANT.

Longing is like the Seed
That wrestles in the Ground,
Believing if it intercede
It shall at length be found -

The Hour, and the Zone,
Each Circumstance unknown -
What Constancy must be achieved
Before it see the Sun!

1298, 1873

🌱 Seed starting was one of Emily Dickinson's gardening tasks.

With constancy of warmth, water, and time, small round seed leaves emerge. The new seedling consumes food from the seed itself, a piggy-back pantry, until photosynthesis gets started.

As children bid the Guest "Good night"
And then reluctant turn -
My flowers raise their pretty lips -
Then put their nightgowns on.

As children caper when they wake -
Merry that it is Morn -
My flowers from a hundred cribs
Will peep, and prance again.

127, 1859

Her propagation efforts weren't always successful. Some weeks after a friend sent a cutting of a flowering plant from Florida, Dickinson confessed, "The beautiful blossoms waned at last, the charm of all who knew them, resisting the effort of earth or air to persuade them to root, as the great florist says, 'The flower that never will in other climate grow.'" (The "great florist" is John Milton, and the quote from *Paradise Lost*.) Rooting a stem is vegetative propagation, creating two where there was one. Unlike the story of Adam's rib, it doesn't take divine intervention for stems to take root—though it seems a small miracle when they do.

Annuals and biennials that propagate themselves, dropping viable seed for the next year, appeal to the little corner of Yankee thrift that inhabits the heart of every gardener. During growing season, free plants pop up that can be enjoyed, moved, or given away. Self-sowers loosen up a garden, the horticultural equivalent of deep breathing. Newly planted gardens can be stiff, arranged in symmetrical groupings or rows. Volunteer seedlings materialize wherever they like the conditions. They add a repeating element to the garden and tie things together.

It takes some practice to deal with this beneficence. It can be nerve-wracking to look at a seedling and decide, sheep or goat? Weed or plant? Working with self-sowers in the garden also reinforces a certain slackness in weeding that may or may not suit your personality. Seeds need time to germinate at the right temperature, so they'll come up all through the growing season. If you're too tidy, if you weed too often, constantly cultivate, or mulch too much, your volunteer army will go astray.

❀ Foxglove was one of the self-sowing biennials that attracted bees and other pollinators to Emily Dickinson's garden.

With biennials like foxgloves, extra patience is required, because they don't bloom until their second year of growth.

Regarding self-sowers, Emily Dickinson once exaggerated for effect, tattling to cousin Fanny about her sister, "Loo left a tumbler of sweet-peas on the green room bureau," she wrote. "I am going to leave them there till they make pods and sow themselves in the upper drawer, and then I guess they'll blossom about Thanksgiving time." Try some self-sowers. They are worth the wait.

Dickinson liked color in the garden. She once wrote that she was "grasping the proudest zinnia from my purple garden." Her floral hues spanned the spectrum, but she seemed to favor the cool end: pink and blue, purple and lavender, plus white for contrast. Thomas Wentworth Higginson gave us a peek at her palette when he wrote to Dickinson:

> *I wish you could see some field lilies, yellow & scarlet, painted in water colors that are just sent to us for Christmas. These are not your favorite colors, & perhaps I love the azure & gold myself—but perhaps we should learn to love & cultivate these ruddy hues of life.*

Perhaps Mattie was remembering flower colors when she called her aunt's garden "a butterfly Utopia." Butterflies are sun worshippers, their bodies waiting to register higher temperatures in order to fly. Especially attracted to bright colors—purple, red, yellow, and pink—they came to the Homestead's garden to collect nectar and lay their eggs. Dickinson wrote of them:

The Butterfly's Assumption Gown
In Chrysoprase Apartments hung
This Afternoon put on -

How condescending to descend
And be of Buttercups the friend
In a New England Town -

1329, 1874

(Chrysoprase is a green gemstone, the color of a monarch chrysalis.)

Whether in a "New England Town" or elsewhere, your garden needs to offer something throughout the season if you want butterflies to descend. Today one often hears of plant-pollinator partnerships, those particular adaptations like milkweed-and-monarch. Nineteenth-century naturalists understood this too. Thomas Wentworth Higginson mourned the loss of the native wildflowers as population and suburbs spread west from Boston. He continued, "and with these receding plants go also the special insects which haunt them."

Choosy creatures, butterflies seek out particular host plants for their eggs and caterpillars. Some hospitable hosts are typical inhabitants of flower and herb gardens; others you might only see in a meadow. Once the caterpillars pupate, withdrawing into their chrysalises and emerging as butterflies, their needs change a bit. They need sun, a water source, and plenty of nectar.

In the same way people select dishes at a buffet by presentation and smell, butterflies will search, after their meandering fashion, for flowers with strong pigmentation and heavy fragrance. They prefer flowers with shapes that lend themselves to easy landings—flat-topped composites like asters and umbels like Queen Anne's lace. Dickinson's herbarium included both, plus host plants like milkweed and butterfly weed, and many nectar sources including hollyhock and red clover.

We know that Dickinson was alert to insect life from her writing and from the memories of a neighborhood boy, MacGregor Jenkins, who played with Austin and Susan's children. You can almost hear her calling out from the conservatory

ABOVE A monarch feeds at milkweed in the Homestead garden.

BELOW The stage in the life cycle of a butterfly determines what it needs to eat.

door. "'Come quickly,' she said, 'if you want to see something beautiful.'. . . [He] followed her and she pointed out a wonderful moth which had broken its chrysalis and was fluttering about the flowers." Had she found the cocoon on one of the plants in the garden?

Dickinson left a prescription for plants, pollinators, and the places they call home.

To make a prairie it takes a clover and one bee,
One clover, and a bee,
And revery.
The revery alone will do,
If bees are few.

1779, undated

In this era of climate change, reverie alone will no longer do. Dwindling diversity is a mounting concern. While Dickinson never heard the term "endangered species," she understood it. During the height of her wildflower expeditions, young Emily had already noticed the change. "There are not many wild flowers near, for the girls have driven them to a distance," she wrote in a letter, "and we are obliged to walk quite a distance to find them." We can add diversity back by reintroducing local species in any ground that we are fortunate enough to have in our care.

So whether you are making a herbarium, a "permanent Rainbow" on your windowsill, or a garden "like the Beach" outdoors, you can start with the list of plants on page 200. Find a reputable nursery or a friend with extra roots, shoots, and seeds. With effort and attention you, like Emily Dickinson, will harvest the pearls that result.

They ask but our Delight -
The Darlings of the Soil
And grant us all their Countenance
For a penurious smile -

908, 1865

Visiting a Poet's Garden

🌱

AFTER LOSING HER SISTER, Lavinia lived alone at the Homestead for another thirteen years until her death in August 1899. She continued to tend the garden. Every fall, Vinnie had the soil around shrubs and rosebushes amended with well-rotted manure from the barn. One year, the hired man informed her that Susan had used all of the "dressing" on her flowerbeds. A friend found Vinnie suffering with anger-induced heart palpitations. A fight over a manure pile? Any gardener can appreciate the true value of black gold.

A different sort of gold flowed from Dickinson's publications. The first volume of 125 poems, published by Roberts Brothers in October 1890, sold out its first run on the day it was released and was reprinted multiple times that year. *Poems, Second Series* followed in 1891. The popularity of the books focused the spotlight on their principal editor, Mabel Loomis Todd. The talented, articulate Todd promoted the poet in readings and lectures. In 1894, she produced a two-volume set of *The Letters of Emily Dickinson*, with a preface including this description of the poet's garden:

> *And the old garden still overflows with annual fragrance and color. Its armies of many-hued hyacinths run riot in the spring sunshine, while crocuses and daffodils peer above the fresh grass under the apple-trees; a large magnolia holds its pink cups toward the blue sky, and scarlet hawthorn lights a greenly dusky corner.*

And then the roses, and the hedges of sweet-peas, the masses of
nasturtiums, and the stately procession of hollyhocks, in happy
association with huge bushes of lemon verbena! Still later comes
the autumn glory, with salvia and brilliant zinnias and marigolds
and clustering chrysanthemums, until "ranks of seeds their witness
bear," and November folds her brown mantle over sleeping flowers.

After Lavinia Dickinson's death, Martha "Mattie" Dickinson—
she later married then divorced Alexander Bianchi, a captain in the
Russian Imperial Horse Guards—inherited the Homestead. Madame
Bianchi leased the house to tenants until selling it in 1916. New
owners, the Parkes, demolished the barn and added a garage. Their
remodeling projects also claimed Emily's conservatory. In the same fit
of renovation, they sand-blasted the light-colored paint from the exterior of the Homestead, uncovering the original red brick—more suited
to the colonial revival aesthetic then in vogue.

The Parkes installed a sunken garden of formal rectilinear beds—
similarly colonial revival—grassing over the more extensive flower
and vegetable gardens that Emily Dickinson had known. They also
built a tennis court at the far corner of the property. Over time the
tidy hemlock hedge grew into a row of trees, was replaced, then grew
into a row of trees again. At some point the ornamental wooden fence
fell into disrepair and was removed, though a gate and a few pickets
were stored away in the garage.

The Homestead has seen significant changes since the poet
lived there. Only a few of the trees that Austin Dickinson planted on
the two properties still stand. An aberrant hurricane tore through
Amherst in 1938. The soils in the Connecticut River Valley were
saturated from heavy rains—eight inches of rain had fallen over
three days. On September 21, the eye of the hurricane moved across
Amherst with gusts of wind over one hundred miles per hour, pulling
root balls of huge trees out of the sodden ground and snapping off
trunks. This meteorological explosion turned Amherst's tree-lined
streets into a maze of fallen trunks.

More than one hundred trees came down on the land surrounding
the two houses. Emily Dickinson's pine trees were lost. "Four black
walnut trees, a rarity in this section, went down, as well as oaks,

maples, spruces, pines, elms, one grand tulip tree and some hickory. These properties probably lost more of value [than] any other one private holding." This poem seems prescient.

The Wind took up the Northern Things
And piled them in the South -
Then gave the East unto the West
And opening his mouth
The four Divisions of the Earth
Did make as to devour
While everything to corners slunk
Behind the awful power -

The Wind unto his Chambers went
And nature ventured out -
Her subjects scattered into place
Her systems ranged about

Again the smoke from Dwellings rose
The Day abroad was heard
How intimate, a Tempest past
The Transport of the Bird -

1152, 1868

Luckily one white oak on the Homestead's lawn survived. It stands sentinel on the southeast side of the Homestead, outside the study and conservatory. Austin chose the site wisely, leaving space for the horizontal branches. Today it spreads over fifty feet across the lawn. The name of the genus, *Quercus*, is thought to be from a Celtic word meaning "to inquire." Emily Dickinson inquired of the oaks as well.

I robbed the Woods -
The trusting Woods -
The unsuspecting Trees
Brought out their Burs and mosses -
My fantasy to please -

The oldest tree on the property is Austin's white oak, growing on the southeast side of the Homestead.

> I scanned their trinkets curious -
> I grasped - I bore away -
> What will the solemn Hemlock -
> What will the Oak tree say?
>
> 57A, 1859

If you look at one of the leaves from a white oak, you will see that it is simply shaped, like a child's drawing. Its leaves are lobed. In winter, the dried oak leaves sometimes splinter leaving only the outline and veins intact. A critic once said that Emily Dickinson's poems "reminded him of skeleton leaves so pretty but *too delicate*, not strong enough to publish." Time proved him wrong.

Amherst College bought the Homestead from the Parke family in 1965. For many years it was a residence for faculty with a designated curator who opened the house for tours on a limited schedule. In 2003, the college acquired The Evergreens and its contents from the Martha Dickinson Bianchi Trust, consolidating the properties under one museum entity.

The Emily Dickinson Museum has been a good steward, calling back the Homestead of the poet's day. The brick is back to the ochre and off-white color scheme that Edward Dickinson chose. The museum is meticulous. A graduate student spent a semester researching the Dickinson fence and gates, measuring remnants from storage, analyzing the paint, and making scale drawings. Reconstructed posts, pickets, and

✿ The restored fence and hedge border both the Homestead and The Evergreens, as they did during Dickinson's life.

gates now span the long edge of the property along Main Street. Close your eyes, and you can almost hear Austin Dickinson's voice ordering, "Boy, shut that gate!"

If you stop by the museum in summer, you may come upon a curious sort of digging. Squares cut out of the sod may be flanked with archaeologists, student interns, and volunteers, carefully scraping and

⚘ According to Edward and Austin Dickinson, gates should be closed.

sifting the soil. Directed by Archaeological Services at the University of Massachusetts, they seek specifics. Where was the exact location of the barn? Was the flagstone walk to the garden ever moved? Along the way, artifacts—relics, if you will—are unearthed, bagged, and analyzed. Results from archaeology and other research methods drive restoration at the museum.

One of the first archaeology projects focused on the conservatory, which from 1916 until 2016 was just a palimpsest on the exterior brick at the front of the house. Archaeologists uncovered the original foundation for the steps. Clues to construction techniques surfaced, including nails from the wood-frame walls and floorboards.

In good Yankee fashion, the Parkes had salvaged much of the conservatory in 1916, reusing the windows for their new garage and storing doors and shutters in the garage rafters. In 2017 the ribbon was cut on the meticulously rebuilt conservatory. A visitor can cross the floor from Edward Dickinson's restored library to stand in Emily Dickinson's "Spice Isles."

The poet's bedroom is the main drawing card for the museum. It also underwent a two-year transformation that began in 2013—the two-hundredth anniversary of the Homestead's construction. Along with Emily Dickinson's original sleigh bed, a small square writing desk and cherry chest stand in their original places, determined by the wear patterns on the floor. Fragments of antique wallpaper discovered under the upper moldings were used to recreate the rose-bowered covering for the walls. The change from the twentieth-century monochrome wallpaper to this bright trellis of purple-pink roses, green leaves, and arching canes has been stunning. Instead of thinking of a white-dressed Emily Dickinson in a room that looked like a blank page, one can now picture her writing in an interior space that looks like a garden.

✿ The poet's room.

The landscape is gradually coming back to something the poet, her family, and their staff would recognize. The tennis court is gone. Trees are well-tended. In 2009, the firm of Martha Lyon Landscape Architecture documented the landscape in reports and action plans. Its first result was immediate. Overgrown and diseased hemlocks were replaced with a new 1,400-foot-long hedge, now pruned and carefully tended. Plans are underway to restore the path between the houses along with Austin and Susan's picturesque landscape garden.

A small orchard is newly planted in the sunny southeastern corner of the property along Triangle Street. "Buccaneers of Buzz" are encouraged to take up residence in an adjacent mason bee house and frequent the bed of pollinator plants nearby. The volunteer orchardist, Francis Martin, has nurtured an older apple tree on the property

Artist Victoria Dickson is one of the volunteers who tend the garden along with Amherst College horticulturists.

back to bearing. He identified it as a seedling offspring of a hardy Massachusetts heirloom, the Tolman Sweet. As apples do not come true from seed—seedlings differ from parent plants—it is unique. The museum organized a vote to christen the variety, resulting in the name Dickinson Sweeting. Now perhaps more will be able to "have a pippin / From off my Father's tree!"

Beyond the boundaries of her father's properties, a time-traveling Dickinson would find familiar and foreign in the Amherst landscape. The street trees are different. Late in Dickinson's life, a sturdy row of young trees was planted in the margin between sidewalk and curb, directly in front of the Homestead. Those are gone. They were American elms, *Ulmus americana*, a favorite selection of Austin and the Amherst Ornamental Tree Association.

Native to eastern North America, the elm was ideal for street use because of its distinctive shape. Its branches grow up and out from the crown, arching like a tall vase, made-to-order for shade above and visibility below. Only a few elms linger in Amherst, survivors of Dutch elm disease. Spores of the *Ceratocystis* fungus, an organism that clogs the tree's vascular system killing its host, spread in a biological chain reaction from a shipment of European elm logs. The spores traveled root-to-root along city streets and hitchhiked with bark beetles, extending their reach. Elms were decimated, a loss to places both urban and wild. It changed the landscape of America, echoed by the chestnut blight, the hemlock wooly adelgid, and the emerald ash borer, to name a few.

Death is like the insect
Menacing the tree,
Competent to kill it,
But decoyed may be.

Bait it with the balsam,
Seek it with the saw,
Baffle, if it cost you
Everything you are.

Then, if it have burrowed
Out of reach of skill -
Wring the tree and leave it.
'Tis the vermin's will.

1783, undated

Yet despite the menaces to the trees, Amherst continues to be a community of shade due to combined efforts of citizens and government, including an Urban Forest Restoration project that, since 2013, has planted over a thousand trees.

You can still stroll to The Dell, David and Mabel Todd's elaborate Queen Anne cottage with its arched front porch at 90 Spring Street. Its shingles are no longer painted red with green trim, the colors that

Mabel chose, but it is still a private home, just a three-minute walk from The Evergreens and the Homestead. At the time, the uninterrupted Dickinson meadow stretched between the two, though the space is now filled with houses and assorted businesses. The gardens that Austin created around The Dell are gone, but at the corner of Spring and Dickinson Streets, you can still find one of the two stone pillars that he put up when the road was laid. That pillar marks what was the southeast corner of the Dickinson meadow.

Another stone structure from the Dickinson era—just up Main Street and a bit closer to town—is the First Congregational Church. Diagonally across from The Evergreens, Austin Dickinson helped oversee its construction in 1867 and continued to work on its landscaping for the rest of his life. His sister Emily never attended this incarnation of the Congregational Church. In her youth she worshipped at the large yellow building topped with a cupola on South Pleasant Street across from the Amherst College. It now houses financial and career offices. Crossing the street and going up the hill to the main campus, you will pass the Octagon, the first college observatory and the building that housed the lectures that Emily attended while a student at Amherst Academy.

Amherst College's Frost Library is named for poet Robert Frost who taught at Amherst from the 1920s to the 1960s. It is built on the site of Walker Hall, a building that once provided an office for David Todd and an art studio for Mabel. The library holds a significant collection of Dickinson materials, crowned by the 1847 daguerreotype and the "fragment poems," written on paper that the poet repurposed. These came to Amherst College as a donation from Millicent Todd Bingham, Mabel and David Todd's daughter. She gave the rest of her mother's papers to Yale. In 1950, Martha Dickinson Bianchi's heirs sold the bulk of their Emily Dickinson papers and possessions to a Harvard graduate who gifted them to his alma mater. These include the fascicles, letters, portraits, some furniture, and the herbarium.

The Amherst College campus shaped by Austin Dickinson, Frederick Law Olmsted, and Calvert Vaux, among others, is much expanded yet well-preserved. Unlike other institutions of higher education, Amherst has resisted the temptation to close off the open horseshoe of its central quad with a new building. Today, standing in front of the Frost Library and looking across the lawn, the vista opens over the War Memorial to the Holyoke Range, encouraging broader thoughts.

The town common in Amherst is a rolling grassy space, with trees on the edges and open lawn in the center. Students study there in warmer months, soaking up the sun. It hosts a weekly farmers' market during the growing season, and a variety of fairs and festivals. Jones Library, the main branch of Amherst's public library system, is two blocks away on Amity Street. Its Special Collections offer a wealth of material about Emily Dickinson and the town she called home. In front of the parking lot directly across from the library is a stone marker commemorating the site of Amherst Academy.

From Jones Library, you can walk next door to the Amherst Historical Society's Museum in the eighteenth-century Strong House. While the museum's hours are limited, it is worth scheduling time to be there if your plans allow. It features Emily Dickinson's actual white dress—the one at the Homestead is an exact reproduction. There are also several displays devoted to Mabel Loomis Todd, a driving force behind the organization of the society. These include some splendid examples of Todd's paintings—botanical and butterflies—and details about her conservation activities in Pelham and on Hog Island, Maine.

There are fewer wild places within an easy walk of the Homestead, though Amherst and surrounding communities have been diligent in preserving open space. Dickinson would recognize various parts of the town trail system and the wildflowers protected in various parks and reservations around "the Valley"—Amethyst Brook, the Notch, Skinner State Park, Mount Holyoke, the Conte National Fish and Wildlife Refuge, High Ledges Wildlife Sanctuary, and the Emily Dickinson Trail that runs along the Ford River. Each year in these preserves, you can still spot flowers that Dickinson pressed for her herbarium, including blooming sweeps of dwarf ginseng. But remember the admonition, "Take only pictures, and leave only footprints."

North of town center is the University of Massachusetts, where you can visit the Durfee Plant House, rebuilt in its original location in the 1950s. Walk a mile to the east from the university, and you will find Wildwood Cemetery, a miniature version of Cambridge's Mount Auburn that Emily had visited in 1846. In his later years, Austin Dickinson laid out Wildwood's winding roads and rolling terrain, a new seventy-four-acre canvas on which to practice the art of landscape gardening. Like Mount Auburn Cemetery, the graves are tucked into a bucolic setting full of choice trees. Austin was buried there next to his son Gilbert in 1895. Susan Dickinson and their two older children were eventually laid to rest in the same family plot. You can also find the grave of Mabel Loomis Todd at Wildwood Cemetery, lying beside her husband and daughter. Carved on Mabel's gravestone are the Indian pipes that she painted for Emily Dickinson.

Emily's grave at West Cemetery is ten-minute walk up Triangle Street from the Homestead. An ornamental iron fence surrounds the Dickinson family plot. She rests between her sister and her parents. The original gravestone is gone, replaced by her niece with a new

❧ Emily, Lavinia, and their parents are interred in West Cemetery.

stone engraved with two words: "Called Back." They are the last two words she wrote, sent to her cousins days before her death. In any season, even on frozen ground, you will often find a flower, a stone, a pencil, or other mementos left by admirers.

At the Homestead, Emily Dickinson could pick out the familiar features of her garden, the way an art historian can spot original shards in a restored vessel. Old granite flagstones still lead down to the garden beds. Austin's oak is magnificent. Many of the plants she knew still grow there. Peonies continue to poke their red noses through the soil each spring. Lilacs, ancient shrubs, bloom every year and continue to attract bumblebees. The last time I worked in the museum garden, monarchs were at the milkweed in two forms—butterflies drawing nectar from the crown of flowers and a caterpillar munching the leaves—oblivious to metaphor but tangible proof of metamorphosis.

Emily Dickinson would recognize her garden.

AN ANNOTATED LIST OF

Emily
Dickinson's
Plants

HERE IS A LIST of her "Darlings of the Soil," the plants that Emily Dickinson grew and knew. It separates those grown on the Dickinson property and documented by the poet and her circle from wild plants that only appear in the herbarium. For those interested in growing edibles, it also separates domesticated fruits and vegetables from ornamental plants.

The table is organized by common name. With the exception of the herbarium and her botany

❧ Emily Dickinson's garden, herbarium, and locale included many different species of *Viola*.

classes, she did not refer to plants by their botanical names, at least not in writing. If you need to find a plant using the scientific name, they are cross-referenced in the index.

- ❧ The column "Botanical name(s)" includes genus and specific epithet where known.

- ❧ The column "Poems" lists numbers from the Franklin edition.

- ❧ The column "Letters" lists numbers from the Johnson edition.

- ❧ The column "Herbarium" lists the page of the herbarium held in the Houghton Library and reprinted in facsimile in 2006. The botanical names identified and cataloged by Raymond Angelo for the Harvard edition are used except when nomenclature has changed since then.

- ❧ The column "Native" is marked for plants that are native to the Northeast.

- ❧ The column "Other" abbreviates references contemporary to the Dickinsons from sources included in the bibliography (see page 234):

AA/PRES = Adele Allen, "The First President's House—A Reminiscence."

BLS/HAMP = Barton Levi St. Armand, "Keeper of the Keys: Mary Hampson, the Evergreens and the Art Within."

JL/*YRS* = Jay Leyda, *The Years and Hours of Emily Dickinson*, Volumes 1–2.

LD/DIA = Lavinia Dickinson's diary, part of the Martha Dickinson Bianchi Papers 1834–1980, Ms. 2010.046, Brown University Library Special Collections.

MASS = *Massachusetts Agricultural Catalogue of Plants, Trees and Shrubs,* 1878.

MDB/*EDIS* = Martha Dickinson Bianchi, *Emily Dickinson International Society Bulletin.*

MDB/*F2F* = Martha Dickinson Bianchi, *Emily Dickinson Face to Face.*

MDB/*L&L* = Martha Dickinson Bianchi, *The Life and Letters of Emily Dickinson.*

MDB/*REC* = Martha Dickinson Bianchi, *Recollections of a Country Girl.*

MJ/*F&N* = MacGregor Jenkins, *Emily Dickinson: Friend and Neighbor.*

MLT/*LET* = Mabel Loomis Todd, ed., *The Letters of Emily Dickinson: 1845–1886.*

PL/*A&M* = Polly Longsworth, *Austin and Mabel.*

SGD/AE = Susan Gilbert Dickinson, "The Annals of the Evergreens."

STORM = Newspaper clipping dated October 1, 1938, in the Jones Library Special Collections vertical file, about the devastation to the Dickinson property caused by the September 21st hurricane.

TREES = *Trees of Amherst.*

❀ Magnolias continued to bloom at the Homestead.

Common name *botanical name(s)*	POEMS, LETTERS, HERBARIUM, OTHER	NATIVE	NOTES
 *Annuals and perennials cultivated by the Dickinsons*			
Baby's breath *Gypsophila*	OTHER MDB/*EDIS*: 2		With frothy white flowers in summer, this tall annual might easily have spurred Dickinson to think of her garden "like the Beach."
Bleeding heart *Lamprocapnos spectabilis*	OTHER *MASS*: 7, MDB/ *EDIS*: 2		An arching plant with dangling heart-shaped flowers. An ephemeral, it disappears in summer to emerge the following spring.
Boy's love *Artemisia*	OTHER *MASS*: 1, MDB/ *EDIS*: 2		A gray-leaved robust perennial grown for its foliage. The Durfee catalog included two species: *Argentea* and *Stellaria*.
Cactus Family *Cactaceae*	POEMS 367 HERBARIUM 56, 64		Dickinson wrote "My Cactus – splits her Beard / To show her throat," so it might have been a type of Schlumbergera, commonly known as Christmas or Thanksgiving cactus.
California poppy *Eschscholzia californica*	POEMS 1442 HERBARIUM 43 OTHER MDB/*EDIS*: 4		Two distinct genera share the common name poppy, and both have a place in Dickinson's herbarium. Bianchi mentioned wild sown poppies in the Dickinson garden, and both California and corn poppies self-sow regularly.
Calla lily *Zantedeschia aethiopica*	OTHER MDB/*L&L*: 53		Martha Dickinson Bianchi referred to this plant as "resurrection calla" in her description of the conservatory. It is easy to imagine Dickinson favoring that name for this white-flowered rhizome.
Carnation *Dianthus*	POEMS 82, 367 LETTERS 235, 279, 585, 882, 962, 969, 1034 HERBARIUM 56, 59		A large genus grown for its tidy, fragrant, and prolific flowers. Dickinson grew a variety of them, though often used non-specific words like "scarlet carnation" to describe them. See "Gilliflower" and "Pink" below for two identifiable species.
Chrysanthemum *Dendranthema*	OTHER MDB/*EDIS*: 2		Bianchi spoke of hardy chrysanthemums in the garden "that smelled of Thanksgiving."
Cinnamon fern *Osmundastrum cinnamomeum*	POEMS 90 LETTERS 213, 394, 472, 506, 696 HERBARIUM 17 OTHER MDB/*F2F*: 39	X	In letters and the poem that include the word "fern," Dickinson does not distinguish among them. Bianchi also mentioned unspecified types of ferns growing in the conservatory. Later in this list, you will find entries for interrupted, rock polypody, and royal fern.
Columbine *Aquilegia canadensis*	POEMS 30 HERBARIUM 50	X	A native wildflower and hybridized garden flower, Dickinson's poem "I sow my - pageantry" suggests that she grew columbine in her flower garden as well as collecting and pressing it for the herbarium.
Corn poppy *Papaver rhoeas*	LETTERS 513, 647 HERBARIUM 32 OTHER MDB/*EDIS*: 4, MDB/*F2F*: 39		Dickinson misidentified this specimen in her herbarium as *P. somniferum*, or opium poppy. The bright red corn poppy is, however, closer akin to her "Poppy in the Cloud" comparison to the sun.

Common name _botanical name(s)_	POEMS, LETTERS, HERBARIUM, OTHER	NATIVE	NOTES
Crocus _Crocus_	POEMS 16, 30, 85 LETTERS 207, 279, 372, 1041 OTHER MDB/_EDIS_: 2		While Dickinson termed the crocus "martial," that was likely due to its upright posture rather than a warlike attitude. Generally blooming in late winter or early spring, crocus are produced annually from underground structures known as corms.
Crown imperial _Fritillaria imperialis_	LETTERS 92		A showy member of the lily family that towers over the spring border. In an early letter, Dickinson compares her friend (later, sister-in-law) Susan Gilbert to a crown imperial, an indication of the regard with which Susan was held.
Daffodil _Narcissus_	POEMS 81, 85, 92, 150, 213, 266, 296, 347, 641, 744, 755, 958 LETTERS 1041 HERBARIUM 57 OTHER MDB/_EDIS_: 2, MDB/_F2F_: 39		Dickinson included six daffodil specimens in the herbarium, arranged with care on a single page. Among them is _N. poeticus_, the poet's narcissus. Their frequent appearance in her poems shows familiarity, if not a preference, for the spring-flowering bulb.
Daisy _Leucanthemum vulgare_	POEMS 19, 20, 30, 36, 41, 63, 72, 75, 85, 87, 95, 106, 108, 149, 161, 184, 238, 256, 319, 363, 365, 367, 424, 460, 985, 1014, 1256 LETTERS 182, 195, 204, 207, 222, 233, 234, 248, 293, 301, 307, 506 HERBARIUM 8		"Daisy" was a sometimes nom de plume, particularly in letters to gentlemen that Dickinson held in high regard. The oxeye daisy, two of which Dickinson arranged to punctuate the eighth page of the herbarium, is an English native brought by early colonists. It settled in the fields and meadows of New England and spread across North America. It is clear from her letters that Dickinson grew some species of daisy in her garden. When she wrote that "Low Daisies - dot," she might have been referring to Bellis perennis
Daylily _Hemerocallis lilioasphodelus_	LETTERS 342a HERBARIUM 26 OTHER MDB/_EDIS_: 2		When Dickinson introduced herself to Higginson with, as he wrote, "two day lilies," they were likely _H. fulva_, according to Judith Farr in _The Gardens of Emily Dickinson_. Bianchi mentioned "old Yellow-lilies" in the garden. One likely candidate is _H. lilioasphodelus_, or lemon lily, a fragrant, long-cultivated species, a specimen of which appears in the herbarium.
Forget-me-not _Myosotis laxa_	LETTERS 499 HERBARIUM 32		This enthusiastic biennial self-sows prolifically, so one can imagine it filling in the nooks of the Homestead garden. When Dickinson proposed an "Antidote to the love of others," she included a sprig of forget-me-not with a note to the Jenkins family.
Four o'clock _Mirabilis jalapa_	LETTERS 294 HERBARIUM 52		Dickinson playfully suggested that the four o'clocks might strike five in one letter.
Foxglove _Digitalis purpurea_	POEMS 207 HERBARIUM 29		If the "drunken Bee" found the foxgloves in Dickinson's garden, then she was their "Landlord."

Common name *botanical name(s)*	POEMS, LETTERS, HERBARIUM, OTHER	NATIVE	NOTES
Fuchsia *Fuchsia hybrida* *F. magellanica*	POEMS 367 LETTERS 279 HERBARIUM 36		While Vinnie's cats occasionally nibbled the fuchsia in the "garden off the dining room," the plants managed to bloom. Dickinson employed their buds poetically, writing that their "Coral Seams / Rip - while the Sower - dreams." These were likely hybrid fuchsia, though the herbarium specimen is hardy to zone 6.
Garden balsam *Impatiens balsamina*	POEMS 1783 HERBARIUM 4		This tall member of the impatiens family self-sows freely. Attractive to pollinators, Dickinson suggested trapping insects using balsam as bait in poem 1783.
Geranium *Pelargonium,* including: *P. domesticum* *P. odoratissimum* *P. peltatum* *P. quercifolium*	POEMS 367, 473 LETTERS 178, 200, 235, 272, 285, 401, 718, 746 HERBARIUM 33 OTHER *MASS*: 3–4, MDB/*EDIS*: 4, MDB/*REC*: 6		Geraniums merited frequent inclusion in Dickinson's letters, likely potted specimens that moved from the conservatory in winter to the piazza in summer. She arranged seven specimens of geranium leaves and flowers on one herbarium page.
Gilliflower *Dianthus caryophyllus*	LETTERS 228, 279 OTHER MDB/*EDIS*: 4		In a February letter to her Norcross cousins, Dickinson itemized "gilliflowers, magenta" in her whimsical inventory of conservatory plants.
Gladiolus *Gladiolus*	OTHER MDB/*EDIS*: 4		While never mentioned by Emily Dickinson, Bianchi remembered them in her Aunt Lavinia's garden.
Grape hyacinth *Muscari botryoides*	HERBARIUM 30		A fragrant, hardy bulb with a tendency to spread.
Heart's ease *Viola tricolor*	POEMS 167 LETTERS 417, 435 HERBARIUM 46 OTHER *MASS*: 6, MDB/*EDIS*: 4		Dickinson's collection of violas in the herbarium included both wild-collected violets and garden pansies like this diminutive species. The garden historian May Brawley Hill identified the young Emily Dickinson's bouquet in the daguerreotype as a bunch of pansies.
Heliotrope *Heliotropium arborescens*	LETTERS 279 HERBARIUM 37 OTHER JL/*YRS* 2: 361, MDB/*F2F*: 4, 9, *MASS*: 4		With fragrant, purple flowers reminiscent of the mouth-watering smell of a freshly baked cherry pie, one can imagine the atmosphere of a conservatory room warmed by the sun and with, as Dickinson described, "heliotropes by the aprons full."
Hollyhock *Alcea rosea*	LETTERS 203, 771, 1004 HERBARIUM 31 OTHER MDB/*REC*: 4, MLT/*LET*		Bianchi mentioned towering hollyhocks against a backdrop of evergreens along the path between the houses. Mabel Loomis Todd gave Emily and Lavinia a hollyhock painting, enthusiastically acknowledged in Dickinson's letter in the summer of 1885.
Hosta *Hosta plantaginea*	OTHER MDB/*EDIS*: 2		This hosta species was popular in the second half of the nineteenth century, when they were known as funkia, or as Bianchi called them, "August Day-lilies." Unlike many hostas, this late bloomer has strongly fragrant white blooms on straight stems.

Common name *botanical name(s)*	POEMS, LETTERS, HERBARIUM, OTHER	NATIVE	NOTES
Hyacinth *Hyacinthus orientalis*	POEMS 367, 967 LETTERS 799, 807, 823, 882, 885, 969 HERBARIUM 45 OTHER JL/*YRS* 2: 361, MDB/*EDIS*: 2, MDB/ *F2F*: 39, 45, MDB/ *REC*: 287, MLT/*LET*		Hyacinths, voluptuous in color and fragrance, appealed to the poet. Dickinson forced bulbs for the conservatory and her bedroom windowsills, grew them in the garden, and sent cut stems along with heliotrope to Mabel Loomis Todd.
Jockey club *Mirabilis longiflora*	OTHER AA/*PRES*		Adele Allen remembered "Jockey Club," another name for the fragrant *M. longiflora*, growing in the Homestead garden.
Lily *Lilium*	POEMS 137, 147, 166, 559, 759 LETTERS 285, 308, 405, 904, 952, 1040 OTHER MDB/*EDIS*: 4, MDB/*F2F*: 9, MDB/*L&L*: 53		If one were to be driven mad by a plant—a "Lunatic on Bulbs" as Dickinson put it—the imbricated structure of the lily bulb and its alluring petals would be a leading candidate. Dickinson labeled one herbarium specimen *L. candidum*, the Madonna lily, but misidentified what was actually the common yellow daylily. Bianchi mentions Japanese lilies, tiger lilies, and Madonna lilies.
Lily-of-the-valley *Convallaria majalis*	LETTERS 163, 901 HERBARIUM 42 OTHER MDB/*EDIS*: 2		Dickinson called them vale lilies, but whatever you call them, their white bells are full of scent. Bianchi related that these flowers were brought to decorate the family graves.
Marigold *Tagetes*	OTHER MDB/*EDIS*: 2, MDB/*F2F*: 39, MLT/ *LET*		Bianchi remembered marigolds rivaling the chrysanthemums for pungency and late-season bloom. While both Bianchi and Todd noted marigolds, they went unmentioned by Dickinson.
Mignonette *Reseda odorata*	LETTERS 279, 286, 478 HERBARIUM 58 OTHER *MASS*: 5, MDB/ *EDIS*: 2		The Homestead gardens included "yards square" of mignonette, according to Bianchi. Known for its powerhouse sweet scent, it must have been a fragrant place indeed.
Morning glory *Ipomoea coccinea* *I. purpurea*	POEMS 214, 470 LETTERS 267 HERBARIUM 21		At minimum Dickinson was familiar with morning glories. The flowers appear in a letter and two poems, though in metaphorical rather than horticultural contexts. The herbarium includes an unlabeled specimen of small red morning glory as well as the more common purple species.
Myrtle *Vinca minor*	HERBARIUM 55 OTHER MDB/*EDIS*: 2		Emily Norcross Dickinson favored this blue-flowered evergreen vine, allowing it to "romp" at will, according to her granddaughter, Martha.
Nasturtium *Tropaeolum majus*	LETTERS 375 HERBARIUM 42 OTHER *MASS*: 4, MDB/ *EDIS*: 2, MLT/*LET*		The nasturtiums massed in Dickinson's summer garden filling it until frost, according to both Bianchi and Todd.

Common name *botanical name(s)*	POEMS, LETTERS, HERBARIUM, OTHER	NATIVE	NOTES
Pansy *Viola ×hybrid*	LETTERS 435 OTHER *MASS*: 6, MDB/ *EDIS*: 4		Dickinson enclosed pressed pansies in a letter to Thomas Wentworth Higginson. Bianchi described the garden "crowded with their faces, impertinent yellow, so solemn black, mauve, purple, and white."
Peony *Paeonia lactiflora*	LETTERS 206 OTHER MDB/*EDIS*: 2, MDB/*F2F*: 39		The beds of pink, red, and white "Commencement peonies," as Bianchi called them, held nasturtiums in summer.
Pink *Dianthus caryophyllus*	LETTERS 235		This ragged-edged pink flower blooms in early summer. Dickinson also called them gilliflowers.
Primrose or cowslip *Primula veris*	POEMS 1422 HERBARIUM 45, 48		Dickinson distinguished primula from cowslips, indicating knowledge of two species of *Primula*.
Snapdragon *Antirrhinum majus*	HERBARIUM 15, 53 OTHER MDB/*EDIS*: 2, 4		Though appearing in neither poem nor letter, Bianchi specifically mentioned snapdragons in her garden club talk. The flower also appears twice in the herbarium, proof positive that the poet knew the plant.
Snowdrop *Galanthus nivalis*	POEMS 79		The nodding snowdrop is true to its season, clinging to winter and disappearing around the time of the vernal equinox. It appears in an early poem, but whether snowdrops made the move from North Pleasant Street to the Homestead is unknown. Dickinson mislabeled star-of-Bethlehem in the herbarium as *G. nivalis*.
Star-of-Bethlehem *Ornithogalum umbellatum*	HERBARIUM 30 OTHER AA/PRES		Only one source mentions this vigorous bulb growing in Dickinson's garden. Use care if you plant it in yours, as it is vigorous and can take over. Its white flowers are star-shaped, inspiring its common name. Dickinson misidentified this specimen in the herbarium as *Galanthus nivalis*, the common snowdrop.
Stock *Matthiola incana*	POEMS 36, 266 HERBARIUM 9		Dickinson's "spicy 'stocks'" are grown for their pastel petals as well as their fragrance.
Sultan *Impatiens walleriana*	LETTERS 235, 655, 676, 677, 746 HERBARIUM 30		Their common name is a nod to the Sultan of Zanzibar, though today we call them impatiens
Sweet alyssum *Lobularia maritima*	LETTERS 279, 286		Dickinson refers to sweet alyssum as bountiful in the conservatory. It is easy to grow in the outdoor garden from seed.
Sweet clover *Melilotus alba*	LETTERS 432, 779, 860 HERBARIUM 13 OTHER AA/PRES		This is a lanky plant with spikes of fragrant yellow or white flowers, unrelated to the more familiar white and purple clover.
Sweet pea *Lathyrus odoratus*	LETTERS 267, 1004 OTHER MDB/*F2F*: 39		Bianchi mentions "platoons" of sweet peas, no doubt trellised on upright stakes or strings.
Sweet sultan *Amberboa moschata*	OTHER MDB/*EDIS*: 4, MDB/*F2F*: 241		A hardy annual with fuzzy flowers in blue, pink, and white. Used as a dried flower.

ANNUALS AND PERENNIALS CULTIVATED BY THE DICKINSONS

Common name *botanical name(s)*	POEMS, LETTERS, HERBARIUM, OTHER	NATIVE	NOTES
Sweet william *Dianthus barbatus*	LETTERS 235 HERBARIUM 59 OTHER MDB/*EDIS*: 2		Did "Papa bring the sweet williams?" One would like to know.
Tulip *Tulipa gesneriana*	POEMS 15 HERBARIUM 43		Two tulips, one in a poem, another in the herbarium, lead to their inclusion.
Wood sorrel *Oxalis,* including: *O. stricta* (yellow) *O. montana* (common) *O. violacea* (purple)	HERBARIUM 45, 47, 16 OTHER *MASS*: 4, MDB/*L&L*: 53	X	Three varieties appear in the herbarium. Dickinson's niece remembered her aunt growing fragrant species in hanging baskets in the conservatory.
Zinnia *Zinnia elegans*	LETTERS 195 HERBARIUM 50 OTHER MLT/*LET*		Todd remembered the "brilliant zinnias" in the late summer in the beds near the Homestead, and Dickinson wrote of one from her "purple garden."

Trees, shrubs, and woody vines cultivated by the Dickinsons

Common name *botanical name(s)*	POEMS, LETTERS, HERBARIUM, OTHER	NATIVE	NOTES
Alternate leaf dogwood *Cornus alternifolia*	HERBARIUM 44	X	Native to the forest edges of New England, this is one of the trees that would have been easy for Austin Dickinson to transplant into his garden. Emily Dickinson pressed two different dogwood blooms as the focus of one herbarium page.
Blue spruce *Picea pungens*	OTHER MDB/*F2F*: 137		Bianchi described her father going out of The Evergreens with Frederick Law Olmsted and Calvert Vaux to inspect a blue spruce "at the extreme end of the grounds." While native to western North America, the blue spruce was only introduced into the New England nursery trade in 1881. Perhaps Austin received an early specimen from one of his contacts at the Agricultural College or from Olmsted or Vaux.
Cape jasmine or gardenia *Gardenia jasminoides* 'Veitchii'	LETTERS 513, 627, 655, 839 HERBARIUM 41 OTHER *MASS*: 4, MDB/ *F2F*: 4, 9, 39, 42–43		What Dickinson called "Jasmin," or in one case, "Jasmine," was the evergreen shrub grown for its fragrant blossoms. She treasured the plant, given to her by Samuel Bowles, and often sent its sturdy flowers to special correspondents including Thomas Wentworth Higginson. A plant too tender to survive the Amherst freezes, Dickinson's gardenia moved from the east piazza in summer to the conservatory in winter.
Chestnut *Castanea dentata*	POEMS 1414, 1670 LETTERS 268, 271, 272, 375, 1041 HERBARIUM 14 OTHER BLS/HAMP, MDB/*REC*: 3	X	Dickinson compared the color of her hair to that of the chestnut burr. Mary Hampson, the sole resident of The Evergreens for many years after Bianchi's death, mentioned two chestnuts of "the kind you eat" in front of the Homestead, removed in the 1920s for the installation of a new sidewalk.

Common name *botanical name(s)*	POEMS, LETTERS, HERBARIUM, OTHER	NATIVE	NOTES
Clematis or virgin's bower *Clematis occidentalis*	POEMS 628 HERBARIUM 16, 36 OTHER *MASS*: 7	X	The species and varieties of clematis offer a range of flower color and habit, including the two North American natives Dickinson included in the herbarium. The poet captured the distinctive clematis seedpods as "Electric Hair." The Durfee catalog of 1878 listed fifteen varieties
Common lilac *Syringa vulgaris*	POEMS 374, 1261, 1547 LETTERS 502, 712 HERBARIUM 51		At least one of the long-lived plants grew close enough to one the Homestead's windows to let Dickinson spot a bee feasting from its elaborate panicles while she was penning a letter on a warm day in May 1877. The setting sun was a "Firmamental Lilac" to the poet.
Daphne *Daphne odora*	LETTERS 513, 637, 980, 1037 OTHER *MASS*: 2, MDB/*F2F*: 39		Daphne was Dickinson's favorite conservatory flower, at least according to a letter she sent to Thomas Wentworth Higginson. Grown in a pot, and moved outside for the summer, its fragrance must have embraced the little glass room.
Elm *Ulmus americana*	POEMS 79 LETTERS 184 OTHER *MASS*: 10, MDB/*REC*: 3, STORM	X	Austin Dickinson and the Village Improvement Society planted elms as street trees in front of the Homestead and The Evergreens.
Flowering dogwood *Cornus florida*	HERBARIUM 44	X	Bianchi mentioned wild dogwood growing at The Evergreens, most likely the flowering dogwood.
Ginkgo *Ginkgo biloba*	OTHER PL/*A&M*: 415, *TREES*: 19		*Trees of Amherst* in 1959 noted the ginkgo at The Evergreens and the Amherst College president's house, "one of a group planted by Austin Dickinson." Gingko grows on at The Evergreens. In 1897, Mabel Loomis Todd listed ginkgo among the "myriad lovely things" that Austin had planted for her at The Dell.
Hawthorn *Crataegus dodgei*	HERBARIUM 31 OTHER MDB/*REC*: 4, MLT/*LET*	X	When Dickinson wrote the word "Hawthorne" in several letters, she was referring to author Nathaniel Hawthorne rather than the ornamental tree. Bianchi noted hawthorns on either side of the front walk at The Evergreens, and Todd described a spot in the poet's garden where "scarlet hawthorn lights a greenly dusky corner."
Hemlock *Tsuga canadensis*	POEMS 57, 137, 400, 710 LETTERS 308, 309 OTHER *MASS*: 11	X	One might imagine Dickinson on a winter day, looking out one of her bedroom windows and writing, "I think the Hemlock likes to stand / Opon a Marge of Snow."
Hickory *Carya*	OTHER STORM	X	Various species of hickory, from the easily identified shagbark to the butternut and mockernut, are native to western Massachusetts, though it isn't known which grew on the Dickinson property.

Common name _botanical name(s)_	POEMS, LETTERS, HERBARIUM, OTHER	NATIVE	NOTES
Honeysuckle _Lonicera canadensis_ _L. dioica_ _L. japonica_ _L. periclymenum_ _L. tatarica_	LETTERS 165, 266 HERBARIUM 4, 7, 50, 52, 62 OTHER MDB/_EDIS_: 4, MDB/_F2F_: 5, MLT/ _LET_		The hummingbird magnet, also known as honey-suckle, is well represented in Dickinson's herbar-ium. The specimens laid out in its pages prove familiarity with native and introduced species of shrub and climbing habits. Bianchi remembered honeysuckle climbing on a trellis "by the east window where the little writing table stood." That plant and those that Emily and Lavinia trained on arbors over the garden path were likely either the Asian _L. japonica_ or the European _periclymenum_. Only _canadensis_ and _dioica_ are native.
Horsechestnut _Aesculus_	HERBARIUM 26 OTHER BLS/HAMP, _MASS_: 10		Mary Hampson remembered a deep pink chestnut at The Evergreens, likely _A._ ×_carnea_ or _A. dentata_. The horsechestnut or buckeye, _A. hippocastanum_, is included in the herbarium.
Japonica _Chaenomeles japonica_	LETTERS 830 HERBARIUM 27 OTHER MDB/_REC_: 91		What Dickinson called "japonica" is what most gar-deners today call "flowering quince." This tall, open shrub is grown for its early flowering branches, though Dickinson wrote a friend in June 1883 that their japonica had produced a rare apple. Her use of "apple" is apt, as the fruits are similar. Japonica and apple share the same branch of the taxonomic tree, being members of the robust rose family.
Jasmine _Jasminum officinale_	POEMS 203, 309 LETTERS 279, 399, 942 HERBARIUM 1		The first specimen in the herbarium, first page, top left, is jasmine.
Jessamine _Jasminum humile_	POEMS 203, 309 LETTERS 279, 399, 942 HERBARIUM 1 OTHER _MASS_: 4		There is confusion about which plant Dickinson called jessamine. Some identify it as _Gelsemium_, the Carolina jessamine, a vigorous yellow-flowered vine that grows to a massive size. Bianchi remem-bered her aunt growing yellow jasmine in the small conservatory. Given the growth habit of _Gelse-mium_, the size of the Dickinson conservatory, and the appearance in the herbarium of yellow jasmine, _J. humile_ seems a more likely candidate.
Lemon verbena _Aloysia triphylla_	LETTERS 212 OTHER AA/PRES, _MASS_: 1		This woody herb with fragrant flowers and cit-rus-scented leaves is a culinary herb also used in herbal teas and sachets.
Magnolia _Magnolia_ ×_soulangeana_	LETTERS 280 HERBARIUM 10 OTHER MDB/_F2F_: 136, MLT/_LET_, _TREES_: 24	X	Bianchi mentioned magnolias on the grounds of The Evergreens. _Trees of Amherst_ cataloged a specimen planted by Austin at the Amherst College president's house. Todd remembered a pink-flowering variety at the Homestead, and listed magnolia among the many trees and shrubs that Austin had planted at her home, The Dell.

Common name *botanical name(s)*	POEMS, LETTERS, HERBARIUM, OTHER	NATIVE	NOTES
Maple *Acer*, including A. spicatum	POEMS 21, 32, 915, 935, 1320 LETTERS 235, 304 HERBARIUM 20 OTHER *MASS*: 10, STORM	X	Emily enclosed a cake of maple sugar in a letter to Austin when he was teaching school in Boston in 1853. Maples are ubiquitous in New England. They marked the seasons for the poet: sugaring in spring, shade in summer, and a blaze of color in autumn. Only one species, *A. spicatum* or the mountain maple, appears in the herbarium.
Norway spruce *Picea abies*	OTHER *MASS*: 11, MDB/ *REC*: 4, *TREES*: 27		This large dark conifer with drooping branches was a favorite of nineteenth-century American landscape gardeners. The Garden Club of Amherst listed a "huge tree" among the specimens at The Evergreens in 1959. Bianchi's recollections include "an unbroken wall of pine and spruce" that created a curtain behind their garden between the houses.
Oak (and acorn) *Quercus*, including *Q. alba*	POEMS 55, 57, 301, 728, 882 LETTERS 88, 417, 654, 801, 919, 976a OTHER *MASS*: 11, MDB/ *REC*: 8–9	X	Dickinson's poems encompass not only oak but acorn, which in one instance she aptly dubs a forest "egg." The largest and arguably most iconic plant at the Emily Dickinson Museum today is a white oak, *Q. alba*, shading the lawn to the east of the conservatory. Planted by Austin Dickinson, its roots go deep, its branches wide.
Oleander *Nerium oleander*	HERBARIUM 40 OTHER MDB/*F2F*: 39, MLT/*LET*		The Dickinsons grew oleander as a pot plant, trans-ferring with the seasons between the conservatory and the piazza. According to Todd, Dickinson sent the poem "We'll pass without the parting", to a friend along with a sprig of oleander tied with a black ribbon. This seems ominous, as oleander is poisonous, but perhaps Dickinson was suggesting that the recipient take care. In the language of flowers, oleander signals a warning.
Pomegranate *Punica granatum*	LETTERS 368 HERBARIUM 32 OTHER MDB/*F2F*: 39		Bianchi mentioned the pomegranate, growing in a pot on the summer piazza, its flowering "an event to us all."
Rhododendron or rosebay *Rhododendron catawbiense*	POEMS 642 OTHER MDB/*REC*: 4	X	Great stands of native rhododendron with appro-priately evergreen leaves still bloom around The Evergreens each spring. Native to further south in the Appalachian range, there are isolated popula-tions of wild Catawba rosebay in western Massa-chusetts. Botanists surmise that these populations were manmade introductions.

Common name *botanical name(s)*	POEMS, LETTERS, HERBARIUM, OTHER	NATIVE	NOTES
Rose *Rosa,* including: 'Baltimore Belle' *R. centifolia* var. *muscosa* (moss) *R. damascena* (damask) *R. eglanteria* (sweetbrier) *R. foetida* (Austrian brier) *R. gallica* 'Versicolor' (calico) *R. ×harisonii* (Harison's Yellow) *R. majalis* (cinnamon) *R. multiflora* 'Grevillei' (Greville) *R. rugosa* (hedgehog)	POEMS 4, 8, 10, 25, 32, 53, 54, 60, 63, 72, 96, 131, 147, 176, 266, 272, 367, 370, 465, 520, 545, 772, 806, 811, 852, 897, 915, 975, 1351, 1374, 1480, 1610 LETTERS 189, 230, 266, 337, 399, 401, 417, 669, 685, 820, 844, 873 HERBARIUM 39, 41, 50 OTHER *MASS:* 5–6, MDB/*EDIS:* 2, MDB/*F2F:* 25, 39, Oral history interview, Jane Donahue Eberwein, 8/3/2018		The Dickinson love of roses seems to begin with Emily Norcross who brought the Greville rose with her from Monson to Amherst when she married Edward Dickinson. Martha Dickinson Bianchi documented roses on the adjoining properties. She listed varieties by their common names, including the species and cultivars listed at left, and described some of their placement and training. According to Bianchi, roses were grown as "rose trees" (standards, perhaps), climbers on "old fashioned arbors," and over a summer house in the Homestead garden. Did Dickinson write some of her lines in this rosy bower? It is a possibility.
Sourwood *Oxydendrum arboreum*	OTHER *TREES:* 26	X	A tree native to eastern and southern states with drooping summer blooms and bright red fall foliage. The Garden Club of Amherst documented a specimen "along the Triangle St. side of Emily Dickinson House" during the 1950s.
Syringa *Philadelphus coronarius*	LETTERS 401 HERBARIUM 50 OTHER MDB/*F2F:* 13		The sweet scent of syringa, or mock orange, was one of the numerous fragrant plants of the Dickinson garden. Its late spring blooms bridged from the scented bulbs and shrubs of earlier spring to the roses and fragrant annuals of summer.
Tree lilac *Syringa reticulata*	OTHER *TREES:* 38–39		This lilac tends toward a central trunk rather than the familiar spreading growth of the typical shrubs. The Garden Club of Amherst documented a large specimen in front of The Evergreens in 1959. Given its age, placement, and Asian origins, it must have been planted by one of the Dickinsons, though which is unknown. Its offspring still grows there on the east side below the front windows.
Tulip poplar *Liriodendron tulipifera*	LETTERS 190 HERBARIUM 61 OTHER *MASS:* 11, STORM, *TREES:* 23	X	This relative of the magnolia is one of the tallest trees of the eastern deciduous forest. "One grand tulip tree" came down in the storm of 1938, and in 1959 the Garden Club of Amherst noted a specimen at The Evergreens was "seen towering above the heavy undergrowth."

Common name botanical name(s)	POEMS, LETTERS, HERBARIUM, OTHER	NATIVE	NOTES
Umbrella tree *Magnolia tripetala*	LETTERS 280 HERBARIUM 10 OTHER *MASS*: 10, MDB/*F2F*: 136, MLT/*LET*, *TREES*: 25		Bianchi mentioned magnolias on the grounds of The Evergreens, and this species still grows there. It looks prehistoric, or at least tropical as everything about it is big, including leaves that are up to two feet long. Surprisingly perhaps, its wild range is the Eastern United States, though further south than Massachusetts. In the 1950s the Garden Club of Amherst noted a specimen at The Evergreens and another in town that had been given to the owner by Martha Dickinson Bianchi. It propagates easily from seed.
Walnut *Juglans nigra*	OTHER MDB/*REC*: 4, STORM	X	The hurricane of 1938 took down "four black walnut trees, a rarity in this section," on the Dickinson property.
White birch *Betula papyrifera*	OTHER *MASS*: 10, MDB/*REC*: 3	X	White birch is one of several species of birches native to the Amherst area including yellow (*alleghaniensis*), gray (*populifolia*), and sweet (*lenta*). They share bark tattooed with horizontal marks called "lenticels" and dropping catkins that fall apart to release the seeds. Bianchi particularly mentioned white birch, arguably the showiest of the local species.
White pine *Pinus strobus*	POEMS 208, 379, 510, 849 LETTERS 212, 360 OTHER *MASS*: 11, MDB/ *REC*: 8–9, *TREES*: 29	X	Pines grew up outside Dickinson's bedroom windows. In the 1950s, the Garden Club of Amherst documented a large specimen with "loss of branches due to hurricanes" with a three-foot diameter on the Dickinson property.

Fruits and vegetables cultivated by the Dickinsons

Common name botanical name(s)	POEMS, LETTERS, HERBARIUM, OTHER	NATIVE	NOTES
Apple *Pyrus malus*, including varieties: Baldwin Bell Flower Early Harvest Golden Sweets Russet Seek-No-Further	POEMS 2, 236 LETTERS 113, 116, 118, 131, 215, 284, 285, 294, 656, 354, 479, 808, 823, 824, 830 HERBARIUM 28 OTHER JL/*YRS* 1: 282, *MASS*: 9, MDB/*F2F*: 4–5, MDB/*REC*: 259–261		Apples featured not only in the Homestead orchard, but also at The Evergreens, where the west piazza was built around one old tree and another sizeable specimen had a platform built into its branches five or six feet off the ground, accessible by a staircase. Dickinson included a specimen of apple or crabapple in the herbarium, but identified it as a wild crabapple, P. coronaria. Note that there are also many letters and poems that mention "orchard."
Asparagus *Asparagus officinalis*	OTHER MDB/*EDIS*: 1, SGD/AE: 15		Asparagus shoots were a delicacy for the Dickinson table in spring. In summer, arrangements of the tall, ferny branches filled the fireplaces in the parlor.
Bean *Phaseolus*, including: *P. coccineus* *P. lunatus*	LETTERS 49, 340 OTHER MDB/*EDIS*: 1		Bianchi described "green satin" lima beans (P. lunatus) and "red and white" pole beans (P. coccineus) growing in the Homestead garden.

Common name botanical name(s)	POEMS, LETTERS, HERBARIUM, OTHER	NATIVE	NOTES
Beet *Beta vulgaris*	LETTERS 49 OTHER MDB/*EDIS*: 2		The red-veined leaves of beets at the Homestead caught the attention of Bianchi. Dickinson mentioned them growing at the North Pleasant Street house, along with beans and potatoes.
Cabbage *Brassica*	OTHER *MASS*: 7, MDB/*EDIS*: 1		Good keepers for the cellar in winter, the Dickinsons grew both purple and green head cabbages. Durfee offered five varieties of transplants in 1878.
Celery *Apium graveolens*	OTHER *MASS*: 7, MDB/*EDIS*: 1		Bianchi told of rows of celery blanched and moved to the cellar. In 1878, two varieties, Henderson's Dwarf White and Boston Market, were listed in the Durfee catalog.
Cherry *Prunus*, including: *P. avium* *P. pensylvanica* *P. virginiana*	POEMS 195 LETTERS 25, 45, 182, 257, 267 HERBARIUM 48 OTHER *MASS*: 9, MDB/*F2F*: 5	X	Morning glories climbed at least one cherry tree, according to Dickinson's letter of July 1862. Bianchi recorded three, lining the flagstone garden path at the Homestead. This was likely a sweet cherry, *P. avium*, native to Eurasia. There is a specimen of the wild pin cherry in the herbarium, though Dickinson identified it as choke cherry or *P. virginiana*.
Corn *Zea mays*	POEMS 223, 344, 862 LETTERS 292, 320, 378, 487, 502, 948 OTHER MDB/*EDIS*: 1		Sweet corn grew in the Homestead kitchen garden. Presumably they purchased feed corn for the livestock elsewhere.
Fig *Ficus carica*	LETTERS 46, 81, 174, 1033 OTHER JL/*YRS* 1: 282, 359, MDB/*EDIS*: 2, MDB/*F2F*: 42, MDB/*REC*: 292		Mrs. Dickinson's figs received prizes at the agricultural fairs and merited mentions in the town newspaper. Bianchi noted their position along the southeast side of the barn.
Gold currant *Ribes aureum*	LETTERS 31, 49, 100, 120, 835 HERBARIUM 32, 65 OTHER LD/*DIA*: July 22, 1851, PL/*A&M*: 278, *MASS*: 11, MDB/*REC*: 61	X	Lavinia wrote her diary entry about making currant wine while the family lived and gardened at North Pleasant Street house. Bianchi later remembered currant jelly from the Homestead. A recipe sent by Dickinson late in her life includes 1½ cups of currants, presumably dried, though they might have come from the grocer. Red currants are native to Europe, while the gold currant is native to North America.
Grape *Vitis vinifera*	POEMS 862 LETTERS 2a, 16, 53, 55, 174, 272, 566, 782, 863, 888 OTHER *MASS*: 10, MDB/*EDIS*: 2		The trellised grapes grew in front of the east wing of the barn at the Homestead, sheltering the figs. Bianchi documented purple, white, and blue varieties used for jellies, preserves, and wine.

Common name *botanical name(s)*	POEMS, LETTERS, HERBARIUM, OTHER	NATIVE	NOTES
Lettuce *Lactuca sativa*	OTHER *MASS*: 7, SGD/ *AE*: 15		Susan's description of her May luncheon menu included "salad from our own garden and hotbed." Durfee offered plants of Boston Curled, Boston Market, and Tennis Ball in 1878.
Pea *Pisum sativum*	POEMS 1482 HERBARIUM 57		The garden pea climbed its way into the herbarium, and while Dickinson's letters and poems mostly omit them, it's hard to imagine them not growing in the garden and appearing on the table.
Peach *Prunus persica*	LETTERS 16, 53, 55, 340, 520, 654, 860, 1019		Frequently mentioned in Dickinson's letters, peaches are not documented elsewhere.
Pear *Pyrus* 'Flemish Beauty' *P.* 'Seckel' *P.* 'Sugar' *P.* 'Winter Nelis'	LETTERS 337, 758, 949 OTHER MDB/*F2F*: 4, 42		Bianchi noted pear trees, planted along the slope in the Homestead garden, and she listed their varieties.
Plum *Prunus domestica*	LETTERS 321, 337, 901 OTHER MDB/*F2F*: 4		Along with the pear trees, Bianchi remembered plums growing along the garden slope at the Homestead. Dickinson noted that her parents' funeral flowers were damson-hawthorns, likely referring to a type of thorny wild plum also known as a "sloe."
Potato *Solanum tuberosum*	LETTERS 17, 49, 58, 682 HERBARIUM 29		The humble potato does not elbow its way into Dickinson's poems, but is mentioned in several letters (though two references are to potato as a menu item) and is included in the herbarium.
Red currant *Ribes sativum*	LETTERS 31, 49, 100, 120, 835 HERBARIUM 32, 65 OTHER LD/DIA: July 22, 1851, PL/*A&M*: 278, *MASS*: 10, MDB/*REC*: 61		The Durfee catalog of 1878 included red, white, and black varieties of currants.
Strawberry *Fragaria ×ananassa*	POEMS 271 LETTERS 31, 279, 471 HERBARIUM 49 OTHER *MASS*: 10		A young Edward Dickinson also mentioned strawberries in a letter to his fiancée. The Durfee catalog of 1878 included twenty-six varieties of strawberries.
Tomato *Solanum lycopersicon*	LETTERS 53 HERBARIUM 30 OTHER PL/*A&M*: 278, *MASS*: 7		Tomato leaf and flower are carefully pasted into the herbarium, and tomato merited one mention in an early letter. Austin wrote to Mabel in July 1878 that Vinnie had tomatoes ready to go into cans. That same year, Durfee offered two varieties of tomato plant: Trophy and Canada Victor.
Winter squash *Cucurbita maxima*	OTHER MDB/*EDIS*: 2		A feature of the late fall garden according to Bianchi.

Common name *botanical name(s)*	POEMS, LETTERS, HERBARIUM, OTHER	NATIVE	NOTES
	Other plants mentioned or collected by Emily Dickinson		
Adder's tongue *Erythronium americanum*	POEMS 1677 LETTERS 23 HERBARIUM 18	X	The yellow flower Dickinson referred to as "adder's tongue" is a colonizing spring ephemeral, sometimes called dogtooth violet (for the shape of its bulb) or trout lily (for its mottled leaves).
African lily *Agapanthus africanus*	HERBARIUM 35		
Agrimony *Agrimonia gryposepala*	HERBARIUM 28	X	
Allegheny hawkweed *Hieracium paniculatum*	HERBARIUM 44	X	
Allegheny vine *Adlumia fungosa*	HERBARIUM 19	X	
American mountain ash *Sorbus americana*	HERBARIUM 30	X	
Arrowhead *Sagittaria latifolia*	HERBARIUM 22	X	
Aster *Symphyotrichum*	POEMS 85, 150, 374 LETTERS 194 HERBARIUM 62, 63	X	
Balsam apple *Momordica balsamina*	HERBARIUM 38		
Barberry *Berberis vulgaris*	HERBARIUM 1 OTHER *MASS*: 11		
Basil *Ocimum basilicum*	HERBARIUM 19		Dickinson misidentified this plant as lavender, so she must have been familiar with it as well.
Basswood *Tilia americana*	HERBARIUM 32 OTHER *MASS*: 10	X	
Bedstraw *Galium tinctorium*	HERBARIUM 49		
Begonia *Begonia*	HERBARIUM 33		

Bellwort
Uvularia grandiflora
   (large-flowered)
U. sessilifolia
   (sessile-leaved)
	HERBARIUM 17, 50	X	

Bengal trumpet *Thunbergia grandiflora*	HERBARIUM 49		
Big-leaf hydrangea *Hydrangea macrophylla*	HERBARIUM 34		

Common name *botanical name(s)*	POEMS, LETTERS, HERBARIUM, OTHER	NATIVE	NOTES
Bindweed *Convolvulus sepium*	HERBARIUM 17		
Blackberry *Rubus allegheniensis*	LETTERS 320 HERBARIUM 6	X	
Bladderwort *Utricularia vulgaris*	HERBARIUM 37	X	
Bloodroot *Sanguinaria canadensis*	LETTERS 23 HERBARIUM 25	X	
Blue-eyed grass *Sisyrinchium montanum*	HERBARIUM 25	X	
Blue flag iris *Iris versicolor*	HERBARIUM 5	X	
Blue gilia *Gilia capitata*	HERBARIUM 30	X	
Bluet *Houstonia caerulea*	HERBARIUM 40 OTHER SGD/AE: 27	X	Susan recalled an outing with Frances Hodgson Burnett when they picked bluet.
Bottle gentian *Gentiana clausa*	HERBARIUM 44	X	
Borage *Borago officinalis*	HERBARIUM 50		
Bunchberry *Cornus canadensis*	HERBARIUM 44	X	
Bur cucumber *Sicyos angulatus*	HERBARIUM 46	X	
Bush honeysuckle *Diervilla lonicera*	HERBARIUM 3		
Buttercup *Ranunculus acris* *R. bulbosus* *R. fascicularis* *R. hispidus* *R. repens*	POEMS 137 LETTERS 288, 436, 653, 901 HERBARIUM 23		An artful collection of five buttercup species graces page 23 of the herbarium. Of the five, only *fasicularis* and *hispidus* are native.
Butterfly weed *Asclepias tuberosa*	HERBARIUM 3	X	
Calendula *Calendula officinalis*	HERBARIUM 2		
Camas *Camassia scilloides*	HERBARIUM 2	X	
Canada mayflower *Maianthemum canadense*	HERBARIUM 48	X	
Cancer root *Orobanche uniflora*	HERBARIUM 24	X	

OTHER PLANTS MENTIONED OR COLLECTED BY EMILY DICKINSON

Common name *botanical name(s)*	POEMS, LETTERS, HERBARIUM, OTHER	NATIVE	NOTES
Candle anemone *Anemone cylindrica*	POEMS 85	X	
Candytuft *Iberis amara*	HERBARIUM 38		
Canterbury bells *Campanula medium*	HERBARIUM 31		
Caraway *Carum carvi*	HERBARIUM 39		
Cardinal flower *Lobelia cardinalis*	POEMS 1193 LETTERS 117 HERBARIUM 20	X	
Carolina allspice *Calycanthus floridus*	HERBARIUM 31 OTHER *MASS*: 11	X	
Catalpa *Catalpa bignonioides*	HERBARIUM 42 OTHER *MASS*: 10	X	
Celandine *Chelidonium majus*	HERBARIUM 20		
Checkerberry or wintergreen *Gaultheria procumbens*	HERBARIUM 28	X	
China tree *Melia azedarach*	HERBARIUM 25		
Clammy locust *Robinia viscosa*	HERBARIUM 28	X	
Clarkia *Clarkia unguiculata*	HERBARIUM 20		
Clintonia *Clintonia borealis*	HERBARIUM 25	X	
Clover *Trifolium agrarium* (yellow hop) *T. pratense* (red)	POEMS 494, 642, 1779 LETTERS 272, 397, 432, 475, 496, 653, 693, 732, 779, 838 HERBARIUM 15		Dickinson's herbarium includes both yellow hop clover and red clover. In Letter 397, she refers to a rabbit with a clover, likely white clover (*Trifolium repens*) in the lawn.
Colic root *Aletris farinosa*	HERBARIUM 19	X	
Coltsfoot *Tussilago farfara*	HERBARIUM 19		
Comfrey *Symphytum officinale*	HERBARIUM 47		
Coralroot *Corallorhiza maculata*	HERBARIUM 16	X	

Common name *botanical name(s)*	POEMS, LETTERS, HERBARIUM, OTHER	NATIVE	NOTES
Coreopsis *Coreopsis tinctoria*	HERBARIUM 36	X	
Cornflower *Centaurea cyanus*	HERBARIUM 47		
Corn spurry *Spergula arvensis*	HERBARIUM 24		
Corydalis *Corydalis sempervirens*	HERBARIUM 48		
Cottongrass *Eriophorum angustifolium*	HERBARIUM 47	X	
Cow lily *Nuphar advena*	OTHER Whicher, *Emily Dickinson: This Was a Poet*, 55	X	
Cow parsnip *Heracleum maximum*	HERBARIUM 45	X	
Cowwheat *Melampyrum lineare* var. *americanum*	HERBARIUM 44	X	
Cranberry *Vaccinium macrocarpon*	HERBARIUM 14	X	
Creeping saxifrage *Saxifraga stolonifera*	HERBARIUM 25		
Crown vetch *Coronilla varia*	HERBARIUM 35		
Cucumber *Cucumis sativus*	HERBARIUM 40		
Cucumber root *Medeola virginiana*	HERBARIUM 19	X	
Culver's root *Veronicastrum virginicum*	HERBARIUM 31	X	
Cypress spurge *Euphorbia cyparissias*	HERBARIUM 29		
Cypress vine *Ipomea quamoclit*	HERBARIUM 16		
Dandelion *Taraxacum officinale*	HERBARIUM 26		
Deerberry *Vaccinium stamineum*	HERBARIUM 19	X	
Ditch stonecrop *Penthorum sedoides*	HERBARIUM 49	X	

Common name _botanical name(s)_	POEMS, LETTERS, HERBARIUM, OTHER	NATIVE	NOTES
Dodder _Cuscuta gronovii_	HERBARIUM 19		
Dogbane _Apocynum androsaemifolium_	HERBARIUM 41	X	
Doll's eyes _Actaea rubra_	HERBARIUM 15	X	Dickinson misidentified this plant as snakeroot in the herbarium. The specimen she collected was the similar-looking _A. rubra_, also known as doll's eyes, for its unique seedpods, and baneberry, for its poisonous qualities.
Downy rattlesnake plantain _Goodyera pubescens_	HERBARIUM 22	X	
Dutchman's breeches _Dicentra cucullaria_	HERBARIUM 5	X	
Dwarf dandelion _Krigia virginica_	HERBARIUM 13	X	Unlike the dandelion common to lawns, this smaller plant is native to North America.
Dwarf raspberry _Rubus pubescens_	HERBARIUM 48	X	
Early saxifrage _Saxifraga virginiensis_	HERBARIUM 17	X	
Eastern wahoo _Euonymus atropurpureus_	HERBARIUM 45 OTHER _MASS_: 11	X	
Elderberry _Sambucus canadensis_	HERBARIUM 27	X	
Enchanter's nightshade _Circaea lutetiana_ var. _canadensis_	HERBARIUM 24		
European brooklime _Veronica beccabunga_	HERBARIUM 31		
Evening primrose _Oenothera laciniata_	HERBARIUM 3		
False beechdrops _Monotropa hypopitys_	HERBARIUM 35	X	
False foxglove _Aureolaria pedicularia_ (fern-leaved) _A. virginica_ (downy)	HERBARIUM 43	X	
False pimpernel _Lindernia dubia_	HERBARIUM 13	X	Dickinson labeled this herbarium species Scutellaria, or skullcap.
False solomon's seal _Maianthemum racemosum_	HERBARIUM 27	X	

Common name *botanical name(s)*	POEMS, LETTERS, HERBARIUM, OTHER	NATIVE	NOTES
Feverfew *Tanacetum parthenium*	HERBARIUM 35		
Flowering onion *Allium*	HERBARIUM 57		There are native species of *Allium*, but the herbarium specimen was not adequate for specific identification.
Foamflower *Tiarella cordifolia*	HERBARIUM 24	X	
Fringed gentian *Gentianopsis crinita*	HERBARIUM 21	X	
Fringed loosestrife *Lysimachia ciliata*	HERBARIUM 11	X	
Frog orchid *Coeloglossum viride*	HERBARIUM 23	X	
Garden verbena *Verbena ×hybrida*	HERBARIUM 47 OTHER *MASS*: 6–7		The Durfee catalog listed 44 varieties of hybrid verbena, including one named 'Mattie.'
Gaywings *Polygala paucifolia*	HERBARIUM 16	X	
Gill-over-the-ground *Glechoma hederacea*	HERBARIUM 29		
Ginseng *Panax trifolius*	HERBARIUM 47	X	
Globe amaranth *Gomphrena globosa*	HERBARIUM 28		
Goldthread *Coptis trifolia*	HERBARIUM 27	X	
Golden ragwort *Packera aurea*	HERBARIUM 42	X	
Golden saxifrage *Chrysosplenium americanum*	HERBARIUM 48	X	
Grass-of-parnassus *Parnassia glauca*	HERBARIUM 13		
Grass pink *Calopogon tuberosus*	HERBARIUM 25	X	
Green algae *Cladophora*	HERBARIUM 36	X	
Harebell *Campanula rotundifolia*	POEMS 134 HERBARIUM 24	X	
Heal-all *Prunella vulgaris*	HERBARIUM 9	X	

Common name *botanical name(s)*	POEMS, LETTERS, HERBARIUM, OTHER	NATIVE	NOTES
Herb robert *Geranium robertianum*	HERBARIUM 17		
Horse balm *Collinsonia canadensis*	HERBARIUM 1	X	
Horseshoe vetch *Hippocrepis comosa*	HERBARIUM 1		
Horsetail *Equisetum arvense*	HERBARIUM 39	X	
Indian pipe *Monotropa uniflora*	POEMS 1513 LETTERS 479, 770 HERBARIUM 32	X	Note that Letter 394 also may refer to this plant. In it, Dickinson claims that it was her "pipe" which Fanny Norcross found in the woods.
Interrupted fern *Osmunda claytoniana*	HERBARIUM 28	X	
Irish moss *Chondrus crispus*	HERBARIUM 30		
Jerusalem oak *Chenopodium botrys*	HERBARIUM 39		
Kerria *Kerria japonica* var. *pleniflora*	HERBARIUM 41 OTHER *MASS*: 11		
Ladies' tresses *Spiranthes cernua* *S. gracilis*	HERBARIUM 30, 39	X	
Lady's slipper *Cypripedium acaule* (pink) *C. parviflorum* var. *maka-* *sin* (yellow)	HERBARIUM 24, 35	X	
Larkspur *Delphinium elatum*	HERBARIUM 37		
Leatherleaf *Chamaedaphne calyculata*	HERBARIUM 36	X	
Leatherwood *Dirca palustris*	HERBARIUM 8	X	
Liverleaf or hepatica *Anemone americana*	HERBARIUM 12	X	
Lupine *Lupinus perennis* *L. perennis* forma *leucanthus*	HERBARIUM 13, 31, 47		
Mad dog skullcap *Scutellaria galericulata*	HERBARIUM 22		

Common name *botanical name(s)*	POEMS, LETTERS, HERBARIUM, OTHER	NATIVE	NOTES
Madeira vine *Anredera cordifolia*	HERBARIUM 49		
Marijuana *Cannabis sativa*	HERBARIUM 11		Yes, it is in the herbarium.
Marsh bellflower *Campanula aparinoides*	POEMS 85 HERBARIUM 8	X	
Marsh marigold *Caltha palustris*	HERBARIUM 29	X	
Matrimony vine *Lycium barbarum*	HERBARIUM 23		
Mayweed *Anthemis cotula*	HERBARIUM 14		
Mimosa *Albizia julibrissin*	HERBARIUM 41		
Miterwort *Mitella diphylla*	HERBARIUM 4	X	
Monkey flower *Mimulus ringens*	HERBARIUM 9 OTHER *MASS*: 4	X	
Moth mullein *Verbascum blattaria*	HERBARIUM 12		
Mountain laurel *Kalmia latifolia*	HERBARIUM 28	X	
Mountain sandwort *Minuartia groenlandica*	HERBARIUM 35	X	
Mullein *Verbascum thapsus*	HERBARIUM 12		
Muskflower *Erythranthe moschata*	HERBARIUM 43	X	
Musk mallow *Malva moschata*	HERBARIUM 4		
Nodding trillium *Trillium cernuum*	HERBARIUM 43	X	
Oakleaf hydrangea *Hydrangea quercifolia*	HERBARIUM 34	X	
Orchis *Platanthera hookeri* *P. grandiflora* *P. lacera*	POEMS 29, 162, 642 HERBARIUM 17, 19, 27, 29, 40	X	As Dickinson wrote, "To him who keeps an Orchis' heart —The swamps are pink with June." (F29) Note that two specimens of P. lacera appear on different pages of the herbarium.
Painted cup or Indian paintbrush *Castilleja coccinea*	POEMS 85 HERBARIUM 38	X	Dickinson called this brightly colored and now endangered plant "Bartsia."

Common name *botanical name(s)*	POEMS, LETTERS, HERBARIUM, OTHER	NATIVE	NOTES
Painted trillium *Trillium undulatum*	HERBARIUM 37	X	
Pale-spike lobelia *Lobelia spicata*	HERBARIUM 26	X	Dickinson misidentified this specimen as Lobelia inflata, or Indian tobacco.
Partridgeberry *Mitchella repens*	HERBARIUM 50	X	
Pasture rose *Rosa carolina*	HERBARIUM 11	X	
Persian lilac *Syringa ×persica*	HERBARIUM 51 OTHER *MASS*: 11		
Petunia *Petunia violacea*	HERBARIUM 39 OTHER *MASS*: 5		
Pinxterbloom *Rhododendron periclymenoides*	HERBARIUM 21	X	
Pipsissewa *Chimaphila umbellata*	HERBARIUM 30	X	
Pitcher plant *Sarracenia purpurea*	HERBARIUM 6	X	
Plantain *Plantago major*	LETTERS 85		In a letter to Susan, Dickinson refers to plantain in the lawn grass, and common broadleaf plantain is the likely culprit.
Purple passionflower *Passiflora caerulea*	HERBARIUM 42	X	
Privet *Ligustrum vulgare*	HERBARIUM 1 OTHER *MASS*: 11		
Pogonia *Isotria verticillata*	HERBARIUM 38	X	
Poison ivy *Toxicodendron radicans*	HERBARIUM 6	X	Misidentified in the herbarium as climbing bittersweet. Perhaps Dickinson was wearing gloves when she handled the three leaves and flowers. Or perhaps she was not susceptible to the irritating rash that poison ivy generally confers on those who touch it.
Puffball *Lycoperdon perlatum*	LETTERS 479	X	Note, like mushrooms, the puffball is biologically speaking a fungus rather than a plant.
Purple avens *Geum rivale*	HERBARIUM 39	X	
Purple milkwort *Polygala sanguinea*	HERBARIUM 16	X	
Pussytoes *Antennaria plantaginifolia*	HERBARIUM 42	X	

Common name *botanical name(s)*	POEMS, LETTERS, HERBARIUM, OTHER	NATIVE	NOTES
Pussywillow *Salix discolor*	OTHER MJ/*F&N*: 121	X	
Pyrola *Pyrola secunda* (one-sided) *P. rotundifolia* (round-leaved)	HERBARIUM 41, 45	X	
Queen Anne's lace *Daucus carota*	HERBARIUM 9		
Racemed milkwort *Polygala polygama*	HERBARIUM 16	X	
Rattlesnake root *Prenanthes trifoliolata*	HERBARIUM 29	X	
Red trillium *Trillium erectum*	HERBARIUM 7	X	
Rhodora *Rhododendron canadense*	HERBARIUM 10	X	
River-pink Unknown	LETTERS 479	?	Plant mysteries remain. The letter to her Norcross cousins which mentions witch-hazel, Indian pipe, and puff-balls, also includes "that mysterious apple that sometimes comes on river-pinks."
Rock polypody *Polypodium virginianum*	LETTERS 472	X	Dickinson enclosed a frond of polypody fern in a letter to Mary Channing Higginson, the wife of Thomas Wentworth Higginson, in 1876.
Rockrose *Helianthemum canadense*	HERBARIUM 8	X	
Rose pogonia *Pogonia ophioglossoides*	HERBARIUM 34	X	
Rose twisted stalk *Streptopus lanceolatus*	HERBARIUM 21	X	
Royal fern *Osmunda regalis*	HERBARIUM 66	X	
Rue anemone *Thalictrum thalictroides*	HERBARIUM 40	X	
Sage *Salvia officinalis*	HERBARIUM 18 OTHER *MASS*: 6		
Salvia *Salvia microphylla*	HERBARIUM 44		
Sassafras *Sassafras albidum*	HERBARIUM 38	X	
Scarlet rochea *Crassula coccinea*	HERBARIUM 29		

OTHER PLANTS MENTIONED OR COLLECTED BY EMILY DICKINSON

Common name *botanical name(s)*	POEMS, LETTERS, HERBARIUM, OTHER	NATIVE	NOTES
Sensitive plant *Mimosa pudica*	HERBARIUM 38		
Shadbush *Amelanchier arborea*	HERBARIUM 28	X	
Sheep laurel *Kalmia angustifolia*	HERBARIUM 21	X	
Sheep sorrel *Rumex acetosella*	HERBARIUM 10		
Sheep's bit *Jasione montana*	HERBARIUM 35		
Showy orchis *Galearis spectabilis*	HERBARIUM 37	X	
Skullcap *Scutellaria lateriflora*	HERBARIUM 40	X	
Smooth hedge nettle *Stachys tenuifolia*	HERBARIUM 22	X	
Spikenard *Aralia racemosa*	POEMS 369	X	
Snowberry *Symphoricarpos albus*	HERBARIUM 48	X	
Speedwell *Veronica serpyllifolia*	HERBARIUM 29		
Spring beauty *Claytonia caroliniana*	HERBARIUM 44	X	
Starflower *Trientalis americana*	HERBARIUM 43	X	
Stonecrop *Sedum ternatum*	HERBARIUM 36	X	
Starflower scabious *Scabiosa stellata*	HERBARIUM 38		
Stargrass *Hypoxis hirsuta*	HERBARIUM 30	X	
Strawflower *Xerochrysum bracteatum*	HERBARIUM 32		An Australian native, grown as a cutting flower, fresh or dried.
Striped wintergreen *Chimaphila maculata*	HERBARIUM 30	X	
Sumac *Rhus*	LETTERS 718	X	Dickinson spells it "surnach."
Swamp candles *Lysimachia terrestris*	HERBARIUM 13	X	

Common name _botanical name(s)_	POEMS, LETTERS, HERBARIUM, OTHER	NATIVE	NOTES
Swamp saxifrage _Saxifraga pensylvanica_	HERBARIUM 39	X	
Swamp vervain _Lysimachia terrestris_	HERBARIUM 20	X	
Tall thimbleweed _Anemone virginiana_		X	
Tasselflower _Emilia fosbergii_	HERBARIUM 21		A plant native to Florida and the southernmost states, this must have been given to Dickinson for her collection.
Threeleaf solomon seal _Maianthemum trifolium_	HERBARIUM 27	X	
Throatwort _Campanula trachelium_	HERBARIUM 39		
Tick-trefoil _Desmodium canadense_	HERBARIUM 48	X	
Tobacco _Nicotiana tabacum_	HERBARIUM 36		
Toothwort _Cardamine diphylla_	HERBARIUM 7	X	
Touch-me-not or jewelweed _Impatiens capensis_	HERBARIUM 45	X	
Trailing arbutus _Epigaea repens_	POEMS 85, 1357 LETTERS 23, 115, 217, 318, 339, 551, 1034, 1037, 1038 HERBARIUM 38, 58 OTHER SGD/AE: 15	X	Referenced by Dickinson throughout her life, this low shrub is indeed punctual, signaling the end of winter. Pink in spring and whitening as it ages, the flower eventually disappears but the diminutive woody stems and evergreen leaves persist year-round.
Trumpet creeper _Campsis radicans_	HERBARIUM 46	X	
Twinflower _Linnaea borealis_	HERBARIUM 42	X	
Valerian _Valeriana officinalis_	HERBARIUM 34		
Venus's looking glass _Legousia speculum-veneris_	HERBARIUM 9		
Viburnum _Viburnum acerifolium_ _V. cassinoides_ (witherod) _V. opulus_ var. _roseum_ (snowball)	HERBARIUM 49, 31, 41		Dickinson collected three species for the herbarium. These include the native maple-leaved viburnum (_Acer_ is the botanical name for the maple genus) and the native witherod (withy, pronounced with-E, is any flexible twig used for weaving baskets and the like).

Common name *botanical name(s)*	POEMS, LETTERS, HERBARIUM, OTHER	NATIVE	NOTES
Violet *Viola cucullata* (marsh) *V. pallens* (white) *V. palmata* (palmate) *V. pedata* (birdfoot) *V. pubescens* (downy) *V. rotundifolia* (round-leafed)	POEMS 94 LETTERS 181 HERBARIUM 46 OTHER MDB/*F2F*: 5		In June 1852, Dickinson sent violets to Susan Gilbert in a letter. Violets grew in the Dickinson orchard and in the fields and forests around Amherst. Six species of wild violets appear in the herbarium.
Water plantain *Alisma subcordatum*	HERBARIUM 22	X	
White avens *Geum canadense*	HERBARIUM 60	X	
White turtlehead *Chelone glabra*	HERBARIUM 38	X	
White waterlily *Nymphaea odorata*	HERBARIUM 32	X	
Whorled milkweed *Asclepias verticillata*	HERBARIUM 25	X	
Winged everlasting *Ammobium alatum*	HERBARIUM 18		A flower native to Australia, generally grown as for a dried flower.
Wild black currant *Ribes americanum*	HERBARIUM 14	X	Dickinson misidentified this specimen as the cultivated European black currant.
Wild calla *Calla palustris*	HERBARIUM 36	X	
Wild geranium *Geranium maculatum*	HERBARIUM 15	X	
Wild ginger *Asarum canadense*	HERBARIUM 2	X	
Wild indigo *Baptisia tinctoria*	HERBARIUM 42	X	
Wild strawberry *Fragaria virginiana*	HERBARIUM 49	X	The wild strawberry is included in the herbarium, but the domestic strawberry is not.
Witch hazel *Hamamelis virginiana*	LETTERS 318	X	
Wood anemone *Anemone quinquefolia*	POEMS 85 HERBARIUM 40	X	
Wood betony *Pedicularis canadensis*	HERBARIUM 49	X	
Yarrow *Achillea millefolium*	HERBARIUM 47		

Common name *botanical name(s)*	POEMS, LETTERS, HERBARIUM, OTHER	NATIVE	NOTES
Yellow-eyed grass *Xyris caroliniana*	HERBARIUM 15	X	
Yellow flag iris *Iris pseudacorus*	HERBARIUM 5		
Yellow loosestrife *Lysimachia vulgaris*	HERBARIUM 35		
Yellow passionflower *Passiflora incarnata*	HERBARIUM 42		

Ribbons of the Year -
Multitude Brocade -
Worn to Nature's Party once

Then, as flung aside
As a faded Bead
Or a Wrinkled Pearl -
Who shall charge the Vanity
Of the Maker's Girl

1065, 1865

AFTERWORD

A GRAY DAY, LATE WINTER, and light from a single lamp illuminates Emily Dickinson's bedroom. I sit opposite a replica of the poet's tiny cherry desk, at a card table set up for the purpose. It is at least twice the size of hers. I wonder whether she thrust her knees under the desk primly, with legs to one side. She was "small, like the Wren," attested to by the dressmaker's dummy that faces me, wearing an exact reproduction of her famous white dress.

On the square writing surface of her desk is an inkwell, a pencil, and some scrap paper. Perhaps she kept good stationery in its small drawer, or maybe her father kept the supply of quality paper in his study downstairs. The fireplace or a stove would have been lit to take the chill off the room. Carlo the dog, her "mute Confederate," could have been here, stretched out on the floor. Or was he relegated to kitchen or barn?

There are books stacked on the mantel. A washstand with a cabinet for the chamber pot. A rocker. Her dark walnut sleigh bed. A paisley shawl. And the cherry chest of drawers where she kept her letters and the poems that brought persistent fame after she had been "Called Back."

Four large windows brighten the room. Two face the street; two flank the mantel. I am looking out the second west window—her desk is at the first. Main Street rises up the hill into the town center. It is raining lightly, and the road surface shimmers. She would have seen the road turn slick with mud. In this season, the bare tree branches reveal the view, though there were some large white pines near the house in her day. The spire of the First Congregational Church, finished in 1868 under her brother's watchful eye, is clearly visible. Perhaps she could make out the office block that held her father and Austin's law practice at the crest of the hill.

Visitors would have come into view as they approached the brick mansion or The Evergreens next door. Emerson, Harriet Beecher Stowe, Mrs. Burnett, Frederick Law Olmsted, and many others arrived to share a meal with Austin and Susan. She could have shifted behind the curtains to stay out of sight or stared boldly out. Invisible or visible, she was present.

Today, there is the drone of traffic, but other than that, little noise. I wonder what she might have heard with a poet's ear. Wind among the pine needles. Church bells. Bird song. Creaking floors. Clocks ticking or striking the hour. Coal shifting in the grate or hissing and popping. Vinnie practicing the piano in the parlor. Her "North Wind" of a housekeeper, Maggie Maher, working or humming. Hired men outdoors, splitting wood or shoveling coal, grooming the horses, pitching hay. A cow lowing. Chickens. A niece, nephews, and their friends, playing on the grounds or calling up to her window in hopes of gingerbread. At 3:55, I hear an audible reminder of now and then. The sound of the train, horn incessant, rumbles over tracks a block or two south. She saw it "lap the miles" and heard its "hooting stanza." Perhaps the Hills Hat Factory across the meadow had a whistle too.

There is a neutral smell to this old house, now sealed and climate-controlled. But there would have been cooking odors, whiffs of smoke and ash from the grates, the barnyard on warmer days. At this time of year, there might have been a sweet overlay—the fragrance of hyacinths, forced in the conservatory and displayed on her bedroom windowsills.

I look up to see George Eliot staring down, full face and serious of mien, from a framed etching hung on the front wall. The author of *Middlemarch* seems to be measuring her effect, her head slightly cocked, listening carefully, one supposes. Directly beneath, a similar portrait of Elizabeth Barrett Browning looks over her shoulder and ringlets with a gaze that burns so brightly it was bound to be soon extinguished. One wonders what George and Elizabeth communicated to the poet working in their company.

Two other color lithographs hang on the walls. Over the fireplace, a country scene entitled "Fishing Party" seems to have stepped out of *Mansfield Park*. A servant dressed in livery is handing a decanter from a rowboat to a man on the shore of a small wooded lake. Two couples gather nearby for a picnic. Dishes are spread out on a cloth, with a pair of chairs drawn up for the ladies. The gentlemen wear top hats, the ladies, soft bonnets. The style of the print is primitive, and it is dated 1827, the work of a woman who has signed it, "Emily." I can't decipher the last name.

Over the bed is a Currier and Ives print of Windsor Castle and its park. Two groups of deer animate the composition. Birds perch in the trees. It is English landscape in the picturesque style. Soft trees frame the towers and turrets of the castle. When I turn to look out the window, I move from England back to Amherst and see the tower of The Evergreens with its arched windows echoing back, and visualize the landscape that Austin and Susan created to surround their house. There were specimen trees, select conifers, rhododendrons, benches, flowerbeds, a summerhouse, all linked by curving paths. A consonant chord rings in my head.

The bright, rose-trellised wallpaper gives a soft pink and green cast to the room. Its background chevrons—little birds' feet—point sideways and lead the eye clockwise from north to east to south to west. That and the large pattern of climbing roses make the walls active. Alive. The canes have no thorns. The roses are in phases of bloom, bud to just opening, fully formed to slightly past prime. Youth and age march toward eternity.

Marta McDowell
February 23, 2018

FOR THOSE INTERESTED IN EMILY DICKINSON and her gardens, there is no better place to spend time than with her own words. The Emily Dickinson Archive (edickinson.org), sponsored by a consortium of educational institutions, offers the reader open access to all manuscript poems including the fascicles and the fragments. The Emily Dickinson International Society (emilydickinsoninternationalsociety. org) is a welcoming organization of devoted Dickinsonians, which sponsors meetings, scholarship, the creative arts, and education on all things Dickinson.

By Emily Dickinson

Bervin, Jen, and Marta Werner, eds. *The Gorgeous Nothings: Emily Dickinson's Envelope Poems*. New York: New Directions Publishing, 2013.

Franklin, Ralph W., ed. *The Complete Poems of Emily Dickinson*. Cambridge, MA: Belknap Press of Harvard University Press, 1998.

Johnson, Thomas H., and Theodora Ward, eds. *The Letters of Emily Dickinson*. Cambridge, MA: Belknap Press of Harvard University Press, 1958.

Miller, Cristanne, ed. *Emily Dickinson's Poems: As She Preserved Them*. Cambridge, MA: Belknap Press of Harvard University Press, 2016.

Todd, Mabel Loomis, ed. *The Letters of Emily Dickinson: 1845–1886*. Boston: Roberts Brothers, 1894, p. 352.

About Emily Dickinson and her Gardens

Allen, [Mary] Adele. "The First President's House—A Reminiscence." *Amherst Graduates' Quarterly* (February 1937): p. 38

Bianchi, Martha Dickinson. "Emily Dickinson's Garden." *Emily Dickinson International Society Bulletin* 2, no. 2 (November/December 1990). Includes a previously unpublished script for a lecture to a garden club delivered by Bianchi.

———. *Emily Dickinson Face to Face*. Boston: Houghton Mifflin, 1932.

———. *The Life and Letters of Emily Dickinson*. Boston: Houghton Mifflin, 1924.

———. *Recollections of a Country Girl*. Unpublished 1935 manuscript in the Brown University Library, Martha Dickinson Bianchi Papers 10:18–19.

Dickinson, Susan Gilbert. "The Annals of the Evergreens," reprinted as "Magnetic Visitors," *Amherst Magazine* (Spring 1981): 8–27.

Farr, Judith. *The Gardens of Emily Dickinson*. Cambridge, MA: Harvard University Press, 2004.

Gilbert, Sandra M., and Susan Gubar. *The Madwoman in the Attic: The Woman Writer and the Nineteenth-Century Literary Imagination*. New Haven, CT: Yale University Press, 1980.

Gordon, Lyndall. *Lives Like Loaded Guns: Emily Dickinson and Her Family's Feud*. New York: Penguin, 2011.

Habegger, Alfred. *My Wars Are Laid Away in Books: The Life of Emily Dickinson*. New York: Random House, 2001.

Jabr, Ferris. "How Emily Dickinson Grew Her Genius in Her Family Backyard." *Slate*, May 17, 2016, available at slate.com.

Jenkins, MacGregor. *Emily Dickinson: Friend and Neighbor*. Boston: Little, Brown and Company, 1939.

Leyda, Jay. *The Years and Hours of Emily Dickinson*, Volumes 1–2. New Haven: Yale University Press, 1960.

Liebling, Jerome, et. al. *The Dickinsons of Amherst*. Lebanon, NH: University Press of New England, 1991.

Longsworth, Polly. *Austin and Mabel: The Amherst Affair and Love Letters of Austin Dickinson and Mabel Loomis*. Amherst: University of Massachusetts Press, 1999.

———. *The World of Emily Dickinson*. New York: Norton, 1990.

Lombardo, Daniel. *A Hedge Away: The Other Side of Emily Dickinson's Amherst*. Northampton, MA: Daily Hampshire Gazette, 1997.

Massachusetts Agricultural Catalogue of Plants, Trees and Shrubs. Amherst: Massachusetts Agricultural College, 1878.

Murray, Aife. *Maid as Muse: How Servants Changed Emily Dickinson's Life and Language*. Lebanon: University of New Hampshire Press, 2009.

Phillips, Kate. *Helen Hunt Jackson: A Literary Life*. Berkeley: University of California Press, 2003.

Sewall, Richard. *The Life of Emily Dickinson*. Cambridge, MA: Harvard University Press, 1994.

Smith, James Avery. *History of the Black Population of Amherst, Massachusetts: 1728–1870*. Boston: New England Historic Genealogical Society, 1999.

Smith, Martha Nell, and Mary Loeffelholz, eds. *A Companion to Emily Dickinson*. Malden, MA: Wiley-Blackwell, 2005.

St. Armand, Barton Levi. "Keeper of the Keys: Mary Hampson, the Evergreens and the Art Within." In *The Dickinsons of Amherst*, edited by Jerome Liebling et. al., 209. Lebanon, NH: University Press of New England, 2001.

Trees of Amherst: A Record and History of Some of the Unusual and Historical Trees In and Around Amherst, Massachusetts. Garden Club of Amherst: 1959.

Wolff, Cynthia Griffin. *Emily Dickinson*. Reading, MA: Addison-Wesley, 1988.

About Garden History

Adams, Denise Wiles. *Restoring American Gardens: An Encyclopedia of Heirloom Ornamental Plants, 1640–1940*. Portland, OR: Timber Press, 2004.

Leighton, Ann. *American Gardens of the Nineteenth Century: For Comfort and Affluence*. Amherst: University of Massachusetts Press, 1987.

Martin, Tovah. *Once Upon a Windowsill: A History of Indoor Plants*. Portland, OR: Timber Press, 2009.

Rutkow, Eric. *American Canopy: Trees, Forests, and the Making of a Nation*. New York: Scribner, 2013.

Stilgoe, John R. *Common Landscape of America, 1580–1845*. New Haven, CT: Yale University Press, 1983.

Sumner, Judith. *American Household Botany: A History of Useful Plants, 1620–1900*. Portland, OR: Timber Press, 2004.

Citations

NUMBERS APPENDED to Dickinson's letters, noted with "L," and poems, noted with "P," refer to the Johnson and Franklin editions respectively.

THE LETTERS OF EMILY DICKINSON, edited by Thomas H. Johnson, Associate Editor, Theodora Ward, Cambridge, Mass.: The Belknap Press of Harvard University Press, Copyright © 1958 by the President and Fellows of Harvard College. Copyright © renewed 1986 by the President and Fellows of Harvard College. Copyright © 1914, 1924, 1932, 1942 by Martha Dickinson Bianchi. Copyright © 1952 by Alfred Leete Hampson. Copyright © 1960 by Mary L. Hampson.

Published by arrangement with Harvard University Press.

THE POEMS OF EMILY DICKINSON: VARIORUM EDITION, edited by Ralph W. Franklin, Cambridge, Mass.: The Belknap Press of Harvard University Press, Copyright © 1998 by the President and Fellows of Harvard College. Copyright © 1951, 1955 by the President and Fellows of Harvard College. Copyright © renewed 1979, 1983 by the President and Fellows of Harvard College. Copyright © 1914, 1918, 1919, 1924, 1929, 1930, 1932, 1935, 1937, 1942 by Martha Dickinson Bianchi. Copyright © 1952, 1957, 1958, 1963, 1965 by Mary L. Hampson.

Published by arrangement with Harvard University Press.

Early Spring: A Gardener's Home and Family

"A meandering mass" and "Ribbons of peony": Bianchi, *Face to Face*, 39.

"Seems indeed to": L59, October 25, 1851, to Austin Dickinson.

"The strawberries are": Pollack, Vivian, ed. *A Poet's Parents* (Chapel
    Hill: The University of North Carolina Press, 1988), 114.
"Tell . . . papa to," "I was reared," and "Tell Vinnie I": L206, late April
    1859 to Louise Norcross.
"With fruit, and": L52, September 23, 1851, to Austin Dickinson.
"We all went": L129, June 26, 1853, to Austin Dickinson.
"Subsoiling": L1000, August 1885 to Edward (Ned) Dickinson.
"Mother went rambling": L339, early spring 1870 to Louise and
    Frances Norcross.
"Everything now seems": *Amherst Record*, February 27, 1857.
"That Month of": L976, March 1885 to Helen Hunt Jackson. The letter
    continues, "Sleigh Bells and Jays contend in my Matinee, and the
    North surrenders, instead of the South, a reverse of bugles."
"In Hyacinth time": L823, early May 1883 to Mrs. J. Howard Sweetser.
"The Snow will": L885, February 1884 to Mrs. Henry Hills.
"That a pansy": L435, circa spring 1875 to Mrs. William A. Sterns.
"Nature's buff message": Jenkins, *Friend and Neighbor*, 121.

Late Spring: The Education of a Gardener
"Professor Fiske will": Leyda, *The Years and Hours*, vol. 1, 32.
"I was always": L492, circa March 1877 to Mrs. J. G. Holland.
"Two things I": Leyda, *The Years and Hours*, vol. 2, 477.
"My Dear little": Leyda, *The Years and Hours*, vol. 1, 45.
"Our trees are": L2, May 1, 1842, to Austin Dickinson.
"Edward Dickinson Esq.": Leyda, *The Years and Hours* 1: 121 quoting
    the *Hampshire Gazette*, September 15, 1847.
"The trees stand": L286, circa October 1863 to Louise and Frances
    Norcross.
"I take good": L165, early June 1854 to Austin Dickinson.
"Besides Latin I": L3, May 12, 1842, to Jane Humphrey.
"We found that": Leyda, *The Years and Hours*, vol. 1, 84.
"When Flowers annually": L488, early 1877 to Thomas Wentworth
    Higginson.
"Even the driest": Higginson, Thomas Wentworth. "My Out-Door
    Study," *The Atlantic Monthly* 8 (September 1861): 303.

"The study of": Lincoln, Almira H. *Familiar Lectures on Botany*
 (Hartford, CT: H. and F. J. Huntington, 1829), 10. Note that Almira
 Hart Lincoln was widowed and later remarried and adopted her
 husband's name, Phelps. You will often find catalog entries under
 Phelps rather than Lincoln.

"That part of": Lincoln, *Familiar Lectures on Botany*, 75. Note that the
 illustration of the corolla was from the 1841 edition of the book.

"I have been": L6, May 7, 1845, to Abiah Root. Note that in Harvard's
 Houghton Library there is a small collection of Dickinson plant
 specimens not included in the herbarium album. Some are from
 Europe, India, and the Eastern Mediterranean, sewn onto sheets
 and labeled by an unknown collector, presumably one of her
 friends who traveled on missionary assignments. Another set is
 comprised of unidentified pressed plants that Harvard mounted
 after receiving them.

"An herbarium neatly" and "You will experience": Lincoln, *Familiar
 Lectures on Botany*, 43.

"There were several": L23, May 16, 1848, to Abiah Root.

"A rosy boast": L318, early May 1866 to Mrs. J. G. Holland.

"The mud is": L339, early spring 1870 to Louise and Frances Norcross.

"Root highly efficacious": Eaton, Amos. *Manual of Botany* (Albany,
 NY: Websters and Skinners, 1822), 446.

"Bowdoin took Mary's": Bingham, Millicent Todd. *Emily Dickinson's
 Home* (New York: Harper & Brothers, 1955), 239, from Lavinia
 Dickinson's letter to Austin Dickinson, May 10, 1852.

"The Apple Trees": L823, early May 1883 to Mrs. J. Howard Sweetser.

"I had long": L458, spring 1876 to Thomas Wentworth Higginson.

"When much in": L271, August 1862 to Thomas Wentworth Higginson.

"Shaggy Ally": L280, February 1863 to Thomas Wentworth Higginson.

"Hills – Sir and": L261, April 25, 1862, to Thomas Wentworth
 Higginson.

"Could'nt Carlo": L233, circa 1861 to unknown recipient.

"I talk of all": L212, December 10, 1859, to Mrs. Samuel Bowles.

"Vinnie and I" and "Carlo – comfortable – terrifying": L194,
 September 26, 1858, to Susan Gilbert Dickinson.

"Carlo is consistent": L285, October 7, 1863, to Louise and Frances Norcross.

"When, as a little": Leyda, *The Years and Hours*, vol. 2, 21.

"Carlo died": L314, late January 1866 to Thomas Wentworth Higginson.

"I explore but": L319, June 9, 1866, to Thomas Wentworth Higginson.

"The lawn is full": L318, early May 1866 to Mrs. J. G. Holland.

"Today is very": L122, May 7, 1853, to Austin Dickinson.

"If we had been married": Leyda, *The Years and Hours*, vol. 1, 4.

"There were three tall": Bianchi, *Face to Face*, 4.

"White-Sunday": Bianchi, *Face to Face*, 5.

"Calvinism is a somewhat": Bingham, Millicent Todd. *Ancestors' Brocades* (New York: Harper & Brothers, 1945), 196.

"The wood is piled": Bingham, *Emily Dickinson's Home*, 239.

"Seeds in homes": L691, mid-April 1881 to Louise and Frances Norcross.

"Vinnie and Sue": L262, spring 1862 to Mrs. Samuel Bowles.

"It is lonely": L340, May 1870 to Louise Norcross.

"I feel unusually": Bingham, *Emily Dickinson's Home*, 283.

"Is not an absent": L824, circa May 1883 to Maria Whitney.

"I have long been": L823, early May 1883 to Mrs. J. Howard Sweetser.

"I send you a little": Jenkins, *Friend and Neighbor*, 126.

"Of idleness and": Bianchi, *Life and Letters*, 60.

"I must just show": L502, late May 1877 to Mrs. J. G. Holland.

"Buccaneers of Buzz": P1426.

Early Summer: A Gardener's Travels

For more information about visiting the historical and horticultural Mount Auburn—still an active cemetery and botanical garden—go to *mountauburn.org*.

"I have been to Mount," "Have you ever been," and "Do you have any flowers": L13, September 8, 1846, to Abiah Root.

"A beautiful flat": *Transactions of the Massachusetts Horticultural Society for the Years 1843-4-5-6* (Boston: Dutton and Wentworth's Print, 1847), 158.

"I attended the Horticultural": Leyda, *Years and Hours*, vol. 1, 30.

"Expulsion from Eden": L552, circa 1878 to Mrs. Thomas P. Field.

"How do the plants": L17, November 2, 1847, to Austin Dickinson.

"At 6 o'clock": L18, November 6, 1847, to Abiah Root.

"Trees show their": Bingham, *Emily Dickinson's Home*, 352.

"Sweet and soft" and "He says we forget": L178, February 28, 1855, to Susan Gilbert.

"One soft spring": L179, March 18, 1855, to Mrs. J. G. Holland.

"The tiny Greville": Bianchi, *Emily Dickinson International Society Bulletin*, 2.

"I quite forgot": L124, circa June 1853 to Emily Fowler (Ford).

"Vinnie picked the": L820, spring 1883 to Mrs. J. G. Holland.

Midsummer: A Gardener's Ground

"I supposed we were" and "They say that 'home": L182, January 20, 1856, to Mrs. J. G. Holland.

"The Northwest Passage" and "She received me": Bianchi, *Face to Face*, 25.

"On one occasion": Jenkins, *Friend and Neighbor*, 91.

"I prefer pestilence": L318, early March 1856 to Mrs. J. G. Holland.

"I went out": L165, early June 1854 to Austin Dickinson.

"Vinnie trains the": L267, mid-July 1862 to Louise and Frances Norcross.

"How is your garden": L235, circa August 1861 to Mrs. Samuel Bowles.

"Why do people": Jenkins, *Friend and Neighbor*, 13.

"White one with": Bianchi, *EDIS*, 4.

"The only Commandment": L904, early June 1884 to Mrs. Frederick Tuckerman.

"Must it not": L824, May 1883 to Maria Whitney.

"The Pink Lily": L308, mid-May 1865 to Lavinia Dickinson.

"The poet knows": Emerson, Ralph Waldo. *The Prose Works of Ralph Waldo Emerson* (Boston: Fields, Osgood, & Co., 1870), 427.

"I bring you a Fern": L472, late summer 1876 to Thomas Wentworth Higginson.

"Then I am the Cow Lily": Whicher, George Frisbie. *Emily Dickinson: This Was a Poet* (New York: Charles Scribner's Sons, 1938), 55.

Late Summer: A Hedge Away

"A Balboa of": Bianchi, Martha Dickinson, ed. *Complete Poems of Emily Dickinson* (Boston: Little, Brown and Company, 1924), 1.

"Could it please": L330, June 1869 to Thomas Wentworth Higginson.

"Are you too deeply": L260, April 15, 1862, to Thomas Wentworth Higginson.

"A large country": L342a, August 16, 1870, from Thomas Wentworth Higginson to his wife.

"Let me thank": L1002, circa 1885 to Eugenia Hall.

"I am from": *Emily Dickinson: A Letter* (Amherst, MA: Amherst College, 1992), 1.

"Of 'shunning Men'": L271, August 1862 to Thomas Wentworth Higginson.

"Garden off the dining" and "Crocuses come up": L279, early February 1863 to Louise and Frances Norcross.

"She tolerated none": Bianchi, *Life and Letters*, 53.

"She let me": Bianchi, *Face to Face*, 4.

"I send you inland": L437, mid-April 1875 to Mrs. Edward Tuckerman.

"My flowers are near": L315, early March 1866 to Mrs. J. G. Holland.

"Her crowning attention": Bianchi, *Face to Face*, 42.

"Vinnie is happy": L969, early 1885 to Maria Whitney.

"All her flowers": Bianchi, *EDIS*, 4.

"I had on my most": Bianchi, *Recollections of a Country Girl*, 288.

"One Sister have": P5.

"I have to go": Leyda, *Years and Hours*, vol. 1, 247.

"Was almost certain": Jenkins, *Friend and Neighbor*, 73.

"I hope the Chimneys": L308, from Cambridge, mid-May 1865 to Lavinia Dickinson.

"It was here" and "When her father": Jenkins, *Friend and Neighbor*, 36.

"A strange wonderful": Lombardo, *A Hedge Away*, 2.

"The men with": Bianchi, *Face to Face*, 136.

"Fresh asparagus": Susan Gilbert Dickinson, "The Annals of the Evergreens," 15.

"I am very busy": L771, October 1882 to Margaret Maher.

"Sue – draws her": L262, spring 1862 to Mrs. Samuel Bowles.

"We have all heard": L851, circa 1883 to Edward (Ned) Dickinson.

"Aunt Emily waked": L711, circa 1881 to Gilbert (Gib) Dickinson.

"Oftenest it was": Bianchi, *Face to Face*, 9.

"She was not shy": Jenkins, *Friend and Neighbor*, 21.

"We knew the things": Jenkins, *Friend and Neighbor*, 41.

"She had a habit": Jenkins, *Friend and Neighbor*, 37.

"Which shall it be": Jenkins, *Friend and Neighbor*, 58. Note that the handwriting in Dickinson's original is now read as "Geraniums or Juleps" rather than "Tulips," as Jenkins transcribed it.

"Old Testament weather": Bianchi, *Recollections of a Country Girl*, 292.

"The Days are": L502, late May 1877 to Mrs. J. G. Holland.

"We are reveling": L473, August 1876 to Mrs. J. G. Holland.

"Today is parched": L723, late summer 1881 to Mrs. J. G. Holland.

"Vinnie is trading": L272, circa August 1862 to Samuel Bowles.

"It was unbroken": Allen, Mary Adele. *Around a Village Green: Sketches of Life in Amherst* (Northampton, MA: The Kraushar Press, 1939), 76.

"The Weather is like": L650, July 1880 to Mrs. J. G. Holland.

"I've got a Geranium": L235, circa August 1861 to Mrs. Samuel Bowles.

"I write in the midst": L1004, summer 1885 to Mabel Loomis Todd.

"Such a purple": L267, mid-July 1862 to Louise and Frances Norcross.

"I cooked the peaches" and "The beans we": L340, circa May 1870 to Louise Norcross.

"Picked currants": Lavinia Dickinson's diary is part of the Martha Dickinson Bianchi Papers 1834–1980, Ms. 2010.046, Brown University Library Special Collections.

"Those who have": Child, Lydia Marie. *The American Frugal Housewife* (New York: Harper & Row, 1972 reprint of the 1830 edition), 83.

"I shall make Wine Jelly": L888, early 1884 to Mrs. J. G. Holland.

Autumn: A Gardener's Town

"It would be best": L294, September 1864 to Susan Gilbert Dickinson.

"For the first few": L302, early 1865 to Louise Norcross.

"The laying out: Leyda, *Years and Hours*, vol. 1, 349.

"I loved the part": Bianchi, *Recollections of a Country Girl*, 17.

"Not to walk": Bianchi, *Recollections of a Country Girl*, 29.

"Speeches were made": Leyda, *Years and Hours* 2: 30.

"Aunt Katie and": L668, autumn 1880 to Mrs. Joseph A. Sweetser.

"For the encouragement": Leyda, *Years and Hours*, vol. 1, 74.

"I think too": Leyda, *Years and Hours*, vol. 1, 129.

"A basket and": Leyda, *Years and Hours*, vol. 1, 374.

"Austin and Sue": L619, October 1879 to Mrs. J. G. Holland.

"Aunt Emily's conservatory": Bianchi, *Recollections of a Country Girl*, 59.

"We go to sleep": L520, September 1877 to Jonathan L. Jenkins.

"*Summer?* My memory": L195, November 6, 1858, to Dr. and Mrs. J. G. Holland.

"The sere, the yellow leaf": from *Macbeth* V.iii. 22–23, is quoted in Letters 7 and 73.

"We are by September": L354, early October 1870 to Mrs. J. G. Holland.

"There is not yet": L521, September 1877 to Mrs. J. G. Holland.

"Evenings get longer": L194, September 26, 1858, to Susan Gilbert Dickinson.

"'Dragged' the garden": L337, late 1869 to Louise Norcross.

"The garden is amazing" L49, July 27, 1851, to Austin Dickinson. Amos Newport was of African descent, the grandson of an enslaved man who had successfully sued for his freedom. Amos worked for the Dickinson family in the 1850s. As of the 1855 census he was eighty years old, living with his wife, Melita Paine Newport, aged sixty-six, and seven others—presumably children and grandchildren—who shared his name, ranging in age from two to thirty-four. He died in 1859 and was buried in Amherst's West Cemetery. The listed occupation on his death certificate was "laborer."

"He is the one": L692, spring 1881 to Mrs. J. G. Holland.

"Flaunted red and": Bianchi, *EDIS*, 1.

"Gentlemen here have": L209, circa 1859 to Catherine Scott Turner.

"Trailed over everything": Bianchi, *EDIS*, 2.

"How the sun": Bianchi, *EDIS*, 2.

"Let Horace save": Bingham, *Emily Dickinson's Home*, 386.

"I am small": L268, July 1862 to Thomas Wentworth Higginson.

"I havn't felt": L1041, April 17, 1886, to Elizabeth Dickinson Currier.

"We reckon – your coming": L272, circa August 1862 to Samuel Bowles.

"The grapes too" and "The cider is almost": L53, October 1, 1851, to Austin Dickinson.

"Aside from": Barry, Patrick. *The Fruit Garden* (New York: Charles Scribner, 1852), 178–179.

"The Aunt that": L1049, circa 1864 to Lucretia Bullard.

"We have no Fruit": L936, September 1884 to Mrs. J. G. Holland.

"Men are picking": L656, early September 1880 to Louise Norcross.

"Hips like hams": L343, late summer 1870 to Louise and Frances Norcross.

"It was so delicious": L438, circa 1875 to Samuel Bowles.

"A mutual plum": L321, late November 1866 to Mrs. J. G. Holland.

"Vinnie sent me": Leyda, *Years and Hours*, vol. 2, 381.

In "Besides the autumn poets sing," Dickinson referenced two other poets: William Cullen Bryant and James Thomson. Bryant was born and raised in Cummington, Massachusetts, less than twenty-five miles from Amherst. In his poem "My Autumn Walk" he wrote, "The golden-rod is leaning, and the purple aster waves." Written in 1864, it is an ode to the season and to the Civil War. Thomson's "Sheaves" are from "The Seasons," an epic poem which includes, "Crown'd with the sickle and the wheaten sheaf, while Autumn, nodding o'er the yellow plain, comes jovial on."

"The plants went into": L948, autumn 1884 to Maria Whitney.

"A lovely alien," "It looked like tinsel," and "It haunted me": L479, circa November 1876 to Louise and Frances Norcross.

"In early Autumn": L746, January 1882 to Mrs. Joseph A. Sweetser.

"Veils of Kamchatka": L685, early January 1881 to Mrs. J. G. Holland.

"I trust your Garden": L668, autumn 1880 to Mrs. Joseph A. Sweetser.

Winter: Requiem for a Gardener

"No event of" and "The Hand that": L432, late January 1875 to Mrs. J. G. Holland.

"I do not go away": L735, circa 1881 to Thomas Wentworth Higginson.

"She was so fond": Bingham, *Ancestors' Brocades*, 8.

"When it shall come": L901, early June 1884 to Mrs. J. G. Holland.

"I wish, until": L207, September 1859 to Dr. and Mrs. J. G. Holland.

"As to playing": October 4, 1841, from Deborah Fiske to Helen Maria Fiske, from Special Collections, Tutt Library, Colorado College, Colorado Springs, Colorado.

"Her great dog": Leyda, *Years and Hours*, vol. 2, 14.

"There were three": Jackson, Helen Hunt, *Mercy Philbrick's Choice* (Boston: Roberts Brothers, 1876), 126.

"The quaint, trim,": Jackson, *Mercy Philbrick's Choice*, 26

"You are a great": L444a, late October 1875 from Helen Hunt Jackson to Emily Dickinson.

"We have blue": L601a, circa April 1879 from Helen Hunt Jackson to Emily Dickinson.

"To the Oriole": L602, circa 1879 to Helen Hunt Jackson.

"One of the ones": P1488.

"Soon after I": Leyda, *Years and Hours*, vol. 2, 361.

"That without suspecting": L769, late September 1882 to Mabel Loomis Todd.

"The man of the household": Bianchi, *Recollections of a Country Girl*, 287.

"I cannot make": L770, October 1882 to Mabel Loomis Todd.

"He was as much": Bingham, *Ancestors' Brocades*, 6.

"I don't like": Longsworth, *Austin and Mabel*, 118.

"Most artistic and beautiful" and "My own place": Longsworth, *Austin and Mabel*, 415.

"My House is": L432, late January 1875 to Mrs. J. G. Holland.

"Days of jingling": L190, early summer 1858 to Joseph A. Sweetser.

"Winter's silver fracture": P950.

"My garden is a little" and "It storms in Amherst": L212, December 10, 1859, to Mrs. Samuel Bowles.

"In Bliss' Catalogue": L689, early spring 1881 to Mrs. J. G. Holland.

"A more civic": L1037, early spring 1886 to Mrs. George S. Dickerman.

"I have made a permanent": L882, early 1884 to Mrs. J. G. Holland.

"For the way": Bianchi, *Face to Face*, 45.

"I wish I could": L807, mid-March 1883 to James D. Clark.

"Haven't we had": L9, January 12, 1847, to Abiah Root.

"Ribbons of the year": P1065.

"Then we all walked": Bingham, *Ancestors' Brocades*, 3.

"In childhood I never": *EDIS*, 2.

"Joan of Arc": Bingham, *Ancestors' Brocades*, 87.

"Publication – is the Auction": P788.

Planting a Poet's Garden

"How few suggestions": L888, early 1884 to Mrs. J. G. Holland.

"The beautiful blossoms": L1038, early spring 1886 to Mrs. J. G. Holland.

"Loo left a tumbler": L267, mid-July 1862 to Louise and Frances Norcross.

"Grasping the proudest" L195, November 6, 1858, to Dr. and Mrs. J. G. Holland.

"I wish you": L405a, undated from Thomas Wentworth Higginson to Emily Dickinson.

"A butterfly Utopia": Bianchi, *Face to Face*, 9.

"And with these receding": Higginson, Thomas Wentworth. *Outdoor Studies Poems* (Cambridge, MA: The Riverside Press, 1900), 68.

"'Come quickly'": Jenkins, *Friend and Neighbor*, 122.

"There are not many": L23, May 16, 1848, to Abiah Root.

Visiting a Poet's Garden

"And the old garden": Todd, *The Letters of Emily Dickinson*, 352. Within this quote, "ranks of seeds their witness bear" is from P122A. Todd's description aligns with Martha Dickinson Bianchi's later lecture notes, though Madame Bianchi would be horrified to see her name linked with Todd's. A multigenerational feud rooted in the Austin–Mabel assignations prevented a complete edition of Dickinson's poems from being produced until the mid-twentieth century.

"Four black walnut": Newspaper clipping, October 1, 1938, Jones Library Special Collections.

"Reminded him of skeleton": Habegger, *My Wars Are Laid Away in Books*, 558.

"Spice Isles": L315, early March 1866 to Mrs. J. G. Holland.

Please note that The Dell, David and Mabel Todd's home, originally stood across the street on the present location of 97 Spring Street. A later owner moved it and built a colonial revival in its place in 1907.

A note on Dickinson's bedroom furnishings. In 1950 Martha Dickinson Bianchi's heirs sold the majority of Emily Dickinson's manuscripts—poems and letters—plus the original writing desk and cherry chest from bedroom and an assortment of personal items including her ring from Otis Lord. The buyer was Gilbert Montague, a distant family cousin and Harvard graduate, who gifted them to the Harvard College Library. So, if you want to see more of the poet's original furnishings, you will have to drive ninety miles east to Cambridge and visit the Emily Dickinson room at Harvard's Houghton Library. Public access is restricted to a once-a-week scheduled tour, or by appointment.

Afterword

"North Wind": L689, early spring 1881, to Mrs. J. G. Holland.

"Lap the miles" and "hooting stanza": Dickinson, Emily. *Poems, Second Series* (Boston: Roberts Brothers, 1891) p. 39, Author collection.

⚘

THE COLOR BOTANICAL ILLUSTRATIONS selected for this book are
the work of three New England artists whose lives overlapped with
Dickinson's.

Orra White Hitchcock (1796–1863), a friend of the Dickinson
family, produced scientific drawings ranging from botany to geology.
Her husband, Edward, president of Amherst College, used her work to
illustrate his natural history lectures and writing.

Clarissa Munger Badger (1806–1899) was a Connecticut artist and
poet, her reputation secured by her paintbrush rather than her pen.
Emily Dickinson owned a folio volume rich with vibrant lithographs
of Badger's work with an introduction by Lydia Huntley Sigourney, a
well-known New England poet of the day.

Little is known about Helen Sharp (1865–1910), a Massachusetts
botanical illustrator, other than she worked for a time as an assis-
tant to Dr. Robert Willard Greenleaf at the Boston Society of Natural
History. She was prolific. From 1888 and 1910—starting just after
Dickinson's death—Sharp produced eighteen albums of exquisite
watercolor sketches depicting over a thousand plants, primarily
New England native species. Many of the wildflowers she painted
also appear in the Emily Dickinson's writing and herbarium collection. After Sharp's death, her body was interred in Mount Auburn
Cemetery, another fact that clicks into place with the broader story of
Emily Dickinson's gardens.

I pay - in Satin Cash -
You did not state - your price -
A Petal, for a Paragraph
Is near as I can guess -

526, 1863

ACKNOWLEDGMENTS

———————————— ⚘ ————————————

FOR AN IDEA GROWING INTO A BOOK, I am forever in debt to Jane
Wald, Executive Director of the Emily Dickinson Museum, and to
Cindy Dickinson, then curator, who conducted my first tour wearing
a nametag that read "No relation." I am especially grateful to Cynthia
Harbeson at the Jones Library Special Collection, Stephen Sinon at the
New York Botanical Garden's LuEsther Mertz Library, Leora Siegel at
the Lenhardt Library of the Chicago Botanic Garden, Mimi Dakin at the
Frost Library at Amherst College, and the archivists and librarians at
Harvard's Houghton Library, the Massachusetts Horticultural Society,
the W. E. B. Dubois Library at the University of Massachusetts, the
Brown University Library, the Horticultural Society of New York,
and Manuscripts and Archives at the Yale University Library. Special
thanks to Marianne Curling at the Amherst Historical Society for
sharing her research on Mabel Loomis Todd and the landscaping at
The Dell and to John Martin and Rudy Favretti who completed earlier
studies of the Dickinson landscape for the museum.

Jenny Bent, agent extraordinaire, you taught me how to write
when I embarked on this project so many years ago. Jane Davenport
and Linda O'Gorman, you were the readers who always wanted it
to be better, then and now. Yolanda Fundora and Sarah Stanley,
you were the artists (wizards?) who made the images sing. Andrew
Beckman and Tom Fischer at Timber Press, thank you for the second
chance, and to the inimitable Besse Lynch, for believing.

Gratitude to the staff and volunteers who have worked with me over the years on the gardens at the Emily Dickinson Museum, especially Karl Longto and Victoria Dickson, to my family who instilled a love of books and words, and to my husband Kirke, without whom this seed would never have germinated.

Kelly Davidson, pages 13, 16, 17 bottom, 51, 53 middle, 72, 74 top, 77, 78, 82 left, 85, 89, 94 left, 101 top, 102 bottom, 105 top, 108, 110, 133, 136 bottom, 145 top, 151, 156, 177, 181, 190, 191, 192, 193, 198, 199

From the Rare Book Collection of the Lenhardt Library of the Chicago Botanic Garden, pages 27, 42 top left, 99 bottom, 123, 126, 149, 176

Library of Congress, Geography and Map Division, pages 17 top, 76, 127

Library of Congress, Historic Sheet Music Collection, page 138 bottom

Library of Congress, Prints & Photographs Division, pages 61, 66

The LuEsther T. Mertz Library of the New York Botanical Garden, pages 15, 36, 41, 45, 48, 70 bottom, 86, 93, 119

The LuEsther T. Mertz Library of the New York Botanical Garden, created by John Kirk in 2010, based on a drawing by Marta McDowell, page 18

Michael Medieros for the Emily Dickinson Museum, pages 144, 165

National Portrait Gallery, Smithsonian Institution, page 158

Norman B. Leventhal Map Center, Boston Public Library, page 74 bottom

Private Collection, page 175

Smithsonian Libraries and the Biodiversity Heritage Library, pages 34, 159

Todd-Bingham Picture Collection, Yale University Library, pages 62, 67, 99 top, 106 top left and top right, 160 right, 163, 167, 172

U.S. Department of Agriculture Pomological Watercolor Collection. Rare and Special Collections, National Agricultural Library, Beltsville, MD 20705, page 145 bottom

All other photos are by the author.

INDEX